Twenty Years of Science in the Public Interest

❖

A History of the

Congressional Science and

Engineering Fellowship Program

Twenty Years of Science in the Public Interest

❖

A History of the

Congressional Science and

Engineering Fellowship Program

Jeffrey K. Stine

American Association for the Advancement of Science

Washington, DC 1994

Library of Congress Cataloging-in-Publication Data

Stine, Jeffrey K.
    Twenty years of science in the public interest: a history of the Congressional Science and Engineering Fellowship Program/Jeffrey K. Stine.
        p. cm.
    Includes bibliographical references and index.
    ISBN 0-87168-532-9
    1. Congressional Science and Engineering Fellowship Program—History. 2. Science—Scholarships, fellowships, etc.—United States—History. 3. Science and state—United States—History. 4. Technology and state—United States—History. I. Title. II. Title: 20 years of science in the public interest.
Q127.U6S754 1994
507'.973—dc20   94-24801
                                                                   CIP

Any interpretations and conclusions are those of the author and do not necessarily represent views of AAAS.

Design by Peggy Friedlander

International Standard Book Number: 0-87168-532-9

Printed in the United States of America

Printed on recycled paper

CONTENTS

FOREWORD *by William T. Golden*   ix

PREFACE   xi

1. **Science, Technology, and the Staffing Needs of Congress**   1
   - Stanford Workshops on Political and Social Issues
   - American Association for the Advancement of Science
   - American Society of Mechanical Engineers
   - The Multiple-Society Effort
   - American Political Science Association

2. **Launching the Joint Fellowship Program**   23
   - The First Class of Fellows
   - Energy and Environmental Policy Concerns
   - Orientation and Placement
   - Financial Demands

3. A Perennial Source of Technical Expertise — 37
- American Psychological Association
- The Search for Foundation Support
- Recruitment of Fellows
- Growing Pains

4. Individual Fellowship Programs — 49
- American Physical Society
- Institute of Electrical and Electronics Engineers
- American Chemical Society
- Office of Technology Assessment
- Society for Research in Child Development
- The Humanist Members

5. Assessing the Impacts on Congress, Fellows, and Sponsors — 81
- The Users of Science and Engineering Fellows
- Personal Experiences
- The Sponsoring Societies

CONCLUSION — 113

APPENDICES 117

    A. Organizations Sponsoring Congressional Science and Engineering Fellows, 1973-1994

    B. Congressional Science and Engineering Fellows, 1973-1994

    C. Congressional Offices and Committees Participating in the Science and Engineering Fellowship Program, 1973-1994

    D. Directors of the Congressional Science and Engineering Fellowship Program, 1973-1994

ENDNOTES 147

INDEX 185

FOREWORD

William T. Golden

Jeffrey Stine's volume is an exemplary case study in the history of science policy as well as the definitive history to date of the Congressional Science and Engineering Fellowship Program. It is cogent in analysis, clear in expression, and comprehensive in its study of available documents and its notable interviews with many of the involved *dramatis personae*. It lacks only direct input from the recurrent discussions at meetings of the board of directors of the American Association for the Advancement of Science (AAAS), and perhaps of other organizations, over the years preceding the birth of the program, since no such official records are known to exist. Nor do we have more than anecdotal recollections of the random musings, responsive to perceived needs, of such greats as Robert Oppenheimer and Charles Lauritsen in the years after World War II and the early days of the U.S. Atomic Energy Commission. Stine's well documented narrative of how two-dimensional ideas were translated into three-dimensional action should provide useful guidance and encouragement to other innovators.[1]

The Congressional Science and Engineering Fellowship Program, now in its twenty-first year under the leadership of AAAS — it is even older if one reckons from antecedent activities of other organizations — has been an outstanding success. It has improved Congressional utilization of science and technology; and it has improved the scientific and engineering communities' understanding of the practicalities of the legislative process.

As with many other socio-political and scientific advances, the initiation and evolution of the AAAS Congressional Science and Engineering Fellowship Program is the consequence of the creativity and tenacity of a few individuals focused on a basically sound idea whose time had come in a politically congenial climate. It is an example of how inertia can be overcome and of how a small crystal dropped into a supersaturated solution can precipitate a solid out of a liquid. Dr. Stine tells the story well.

Currently, in the 1993-94 fellowship year, some 30 Science and Engineering Fellows are serving in Congressional offices. Of this incumbent group, 18 are men and 12 are women. Six are employed in Representatives' offices, eleven in the offices of Senators, ten with committees of the House and Senate, and three with the Office of Technology Assessment (OTA), a Congressional service agency. Eighteen, or 60 percent of the group, came from academia; nine (30 percent) from the private sector; and three (10 percent) from government. The selection process for these one-year fellowships has always been rigorous. Only a fraction of the applicants is chosen. In 1993-94, AAAS had close to 200 applicants for its two fellowship slots.

Of the 506 former fellows, 326 are men and 180 are women: 141 served with a Representative, 141 with a Senator, 164 with a Committee, and 64 with OTA. (The numbers add to more than 506 because several fellows transferred from one office or committee to another during their terms.) Approximately one-third of these fellows remained in positions with the federal government (either on Congressional staffs or in the Executive Branch) following completion of their fellowships, another third used the fellowship as a stepping stone to a new position, and the remaining one-third returned to their former organizations. Useful rosters are provided in Dr. Stine's appendices.

Dr. Stine, who was himself a Congressional Science and Engineering Fellow some ten years ago, is a practical historian of science policy. He has performed a service, useful in itself, that establishes a standard for science policy history that should edify scholars and inspire activists.

PREFACE

In September 1993, the Congressional Science and Engineering Fellowship Program marked its 20th anniversary. During the program's first two decades, 40 professional organizations sponsored more than 500 scientists and engineers who worked as Fellows on the staffs of more than 200 personal and committee offices in the House and Senate, and within the Congressional Budget Office, the Congressional Caucus for Women's Issues, the Congressional Research Service, and the Office of Technology Assessment. From the beginning, the American Association for the Advancement of Science (AAAS) has administered the multi-society effort.

Throughout the program's history, its rationale has changed only slightly from the reasons that underpinned its creation. The post-World War II expansion of research and development meant that the U.S. Congress, like legislative bodies elsewhere in the world, increasingly considered matters of public policy that contained significant components of science and technology. Because people conversant with, or trained in, science and engineering had rarely joined legislative staffs, the institution had become overly reliant on the executive branch and lobbyists as sources of information and advice. Scientific and engineering societies, too, were changing—both in articulating their responsibility to contribute to the public good and in sensing a need to learn more about the political process that affected every part of their work.

Aside from fulfilling these goals, the congressional fellowship program has also served another important purpose: training scientists and engineers in how to participate effectively in policy-making within universities, industry, and local and state government, and at the national level. Moreover, Fellows have made significant contributions to the work of the U.S. Congress, sometimes at the microlevel of staff assistance, but also by involvement in a broad spectrum of science- and technology-related issues associated with legislative authorization, appropriation, and oversight activities.[1]

As part of its commemoration of the fellowship's 20th anniversary, the AAAS Directorate for Science and Policy Programs asked me to write a history of the program. Having served as an American Historical Association Congressional Fellow some 10 years ago, I was delighted to have the opportunity to contribute, and luckily this invitation coincided with my being awarded a Smithsonian Institution Regents' Publication Program grant, which gave me the time also to complete this project.

I am grateful to Nancy Pace for conducting the initial research for this history and to David C. Frank and Marc A. Suchard for verifying facts at a later stage in the project. I also want to thank Celia McEnaney for shepharding this book through all stages of production. Michele L. Aldrich and Claudia J. Sturges gave invaluable guidance in identifying and making available the extensive records maintained within the various offices of AAAS and its archives. Richard A. Baker arranged for my use of the Senate Library in the Capitol and, together with Donald A. Ritchie, directed me through the reference files in the Senate History Office. William T. Golden and Joel R. Primack sent me documents from their personal files pertaining to the program's conceptualization, while James Roan of the National Museum of American History Branch Library provided essential assistance in tracking down published materials from around the country.

The American Chemical Society granted full access to the fellowship records in its Washington, D.C., headquarters, while the American Physical Society and the American Political Science Association duplicated pertinent documents from their central offices in New York City and Washington, D.C., respectively. I examined fellowship materials in the active files at the American Historical Association's (AHA) Washington, D.C., headquarters, as well as in the AHA's retired files, which are available to researchers at the Manuscript Division of the Library of Congress. The AHA records were supplemented by documents in the Melvin Kranzberg Papers at the National Museum of American History Archives Center.

Many people gave generously of their time to discuss the fellowship program and the general issue of providing technical staff assistance to Congress. These people included John Andelin, Nancy

Carson, Patricia Garfinkel, Stanley Goldberg, William T. Golden, Ezra Heitowit, John D. Holmfeld, Marcel C. LaFollette, Alan McGowan, Stephen D. Nelson, William Norris, Joel R. Primack, Stephen T. Quigley, J. Thomas Ratchford, Donald A. Ritchie, Richard A. Scribner, Claudia J. Sturges, Albert H. Teich, and Michael L. Telson.

I owe a great deal of thanks to the following people for improving the manuscript through their critical reading of earlier drafts: Michele L. Aldrich, John Andelin, Jon B. Eklund, Paul Forman, William T. Golden, Marcel C. LaFollette, Stephen D. Nelson, Joel R. Primack, J. Thomas Ratchford, Marc Rothenberg, Richard A. Scribner, Claudia J. Sturges, Albert H. Teich, Michael L. Telson, Zuoyue Wang, and William G. Wells, Jr.

Finally, I dedicate this book to A. Hunter Dupree and Melvin Kranzberg, historians of American science and technology known for the quality of their scholarship, the generosity of their professional and public service, and their unfailing integrity.

CHAPTER 1

Science, Technology, and the Staffing Needs of Congress

The Congressional Science and Engineering Fellowship Program was created in the midst of a tumultuous period in the United States. The social ferment associated with urban riots, political assassinations, student revolts, anti-war protests, and movements for civil, women's, and consumer rights found large segments of the nation questioning authority. Although public confidence in science and technology remained solid, scientists and engineers themselves did not draw back from social and political reassessment. At the beginning of the 1960s, scientific and engineering research projects enjoyed considerable government support, much of it spurred by reaction to the Soviet earth satellite, *Sputnik*, which had been launched in 1957. There was a widely shared enthusiasm that scientists and engineers held the key to national security, economic growth and prosperity, and social advancement as a whole. Federal allocations for research and development (R&D) were generously increasing in agency after agency, from the National Science Foundation (NSF) to the Department of Agriculture, from the National Aeronautics and Space Administration (NASA) to the National Institutes of Health, from the Department of Defense (DOD) to the Department of the Interior.[1]

Ten years later, in 1970, scientific and engineering communities had begun to feel far less secure in their relationships to the federal government. This uneasiness was exacerbated by widespread questioning of established values and general disillusionment with the political process itself. Various trends—for example, the leveling off of federal R&D expenditures; evolving national political issues (such as environmental pollution) that had significant technical components; and reassessment of Defense Department support of science (exemplified by the "March 4" demonstrations and the Mansfield Amendment, both in 1969)—contributed to a sense that decisions on important public policy were being made without the input of sound technical advice. This concern about the overall health of and prospects for science and engineering enterprises and their general relations with society intensified in the early 1970s as the authority of science was further questioned, along with the manner in which R&D expenditures were allocated. Science for the People, Public Interest Research Groups, Earth Day, national debates over the supersonic transport (SST) and the antiballistic missile (ABM), Richard Nixon's elimination of the President's Science Advisory Committee (PSAC) and the White House Office of Science and Technology (OST), and the technology assessment and appropriate technology movements all contributed to this climate of discontent within science and engineering.[2]

Conservatives within the scientific and engineering communities looked for ways to buttress public confidence in their enterprises and to assure continued growth in federal R&D expenditures—that is, to urge the public to have more confidence in science and technology. Reform-minded members of the scientific and engineering communities, on the other hand, argued for increased social responsibility among scientists and engineers; they urged that science and technology be made more relevant and that scientists assess their fundamental contributions to the betterment of society. This latter point found expression in various initiatives to enhance the science and technology advice available to the government at various levels. The humiliation and frustration of being kicked out of the White House led many within the leadership ranks of the science and engineering communities to look for alternative mechanisms to provide the highest levels of government with reasoned, expert advice on technical matters. With the executive office of the President temporarily closed, the legislative branch—which the scientists and engineers had largely eschewed in their enthusiasm to communicate with the chief executive and the top echelons of the executive branch agencies—came to be seen as an important avenue of access.[3]

Although Congress came to draw greater attention during the early 1970s, concern about the general relationship between the legislative branch and science and technology had been voiced periodically since World War II, when the federal government began a vast expansion of its patronage of research and development. Within Congress itself, legislators in 1959 had created committees dedicated to science and technology. Increasing R&D budgets to NASA, NSF, DOD, and other agencies led Congress to expand its oversight of programs with significant science and engineering content.[4] For example, as Congress asserted leadership in the area of environmental protection in response to constituent concerns over environmental quality, it enacted a flurry of environmental legislation.[5]

Political scientists and congressional reformers had also become increasingly concerned with the growing dependence of Congress on data and expertise provided by the executive branch. For the legislative branch to play the kind of independent role envisioned by the framers of the U.S. Constitution, these scientists and reformers argued, Congress needed to strengthen the technical capabilities of its professional staff. The alternative, according to this line of thinking, was to suffer under the complete dominance of the executive branch, thereby undermining the inherent power and stability of the separation of powers concept. Political scientist Nelson W. Polsby addressed these concerns in a 1969 article, in which he questioned the traditional practice of appointing staff based on patronage and loyalty. He claimed that "unswerving loyalty to the chairman is seldom enough to produce technically advanced criticism of executive proposals, sophisticated insight into alternatives, or sensitive awareness of emerging problems in the world. Yet these are what Congress needs." He called on congressional members to "professionalize their own committee staffs, thereby increasing the efficiency of their explicit analytical activities and enhancing their own knowledge and power."[6]

The spirit of reform that had been expressed in many quarters of society had also attracted sizable numbers of young (and some not so young) scientists and engineers, who began voicing their concerns for the social responsibility of their own professions. Contributions of scientists and engineers to military weapons (such as Agent Orange) and to projects and products harmful to the natural environment drew the most active participation among the technical community.[7]

As the nation's largest scientific organization (then more than 125,000 members), the American Association for the Advancement of Science (AAAS) found itself inescapably buffeted by the concerns of the late 1960s and early 1970s. Some of the association's more activist board of directors members urged a critical reassessment of the organization. Even the more conservative board members could not help but notice the turmoil within even university science and engineering departments, or the increased restlessness among graduate students and young researchers, many of whom had raised their voices in protest at the association's annual meetings. So sensitized, the AAAS's board of directors issued a resolution in October 1969 calling for the association to dedicate itself in the coming decade "to a major increase in the scale and effectiveness of its work on the chief contemporary problems concerning the mutual relations of science, technology, and social change, including the uses of science and technology in the promotion of human welfare."[8] *Science* magazine reporter Philip M. Boffey became fascinated with the changes induced by these initiatives. "Just what the AAAS *should* be and *should* do has become a matter of considerable debate and speculation over the past year or so," he wrote in April 1971. "The debate has been fueled by a feeling that the AAAS currently stands at a potentially important crossroads in its institutional development."[9] When Dael Wolfle retired as the association's executive officer after 16 years of service, the reform mandate was passed on to his successor, William Bevan, Jr., the 48-year-old provost of Johns Hopkins University.[10]

Although the real push for reform came from AAAS's elected (and unpaid) leadership, execution of the programmatic and structural changes necessarily came from the association's full-time staff. In this respect, Bevan played a central role. He was especially comfortable with the expansion of the organization's public participation and supportive of his staff's trying to implement that expansion. As he stated in 1971, AAAS has "the potential for being the most effective broker of scientific talent in the country today."[11] To focus the association's reorientation, Bevan created the Office of Science and Society and recruited a young physicist, Richard A. Scribner, to head it.

Bevan used the occasion of AAAS's 125th anniversary in 1973 to popularize the association's internal reforms within the general membership. His staff organized a wide array of public programs, some intended to reflect upon the association's past accomplishments and some of which looked toward the association's future. Although not a specific offshoot of those celebratory activities, the Congressional Science and Engineering Fellowship Program—a coalition of science and engineering societies working under the aegis of AAAS's administrative hand—was launched that year with great hope and expectations, as it embodied many of the goals the association had set for itself with regard to expanding the role of scientists and engineers in the public discourse over national policy making. The background of that enterprise, however, involved the ideas and plans of many people from several organizations.

Stanford Workshops on Political and Social Issues

During the year 1969-70, concern about the social responsibility of scientists and engineers was expressed with great vigor and optimism at Stanford University within its newly organized Stanford Workshops on Political and Social Issues (SWOPSI). These student-organized workshops provided an alternative educational forum (accompanied by full academic credit) that encouraged undergraduates, graduate students, and faculty members from across the disciplines to study and address the nation's most pressing social problems.[12] One of the first year's 22 workshops focused on the politics of technical decision making, especially the governmental advisory role played by scientists and engineers. Frank von Hippel, then an assistant professor at Stanford and researcher at the Lawrence Radiation Laboratory, and Joel R. Primack, then an advanced graduate student in physics at Stanford, headed the workshop's task force on congressional decision making. Task force members based their analysis and recommendations on data gathered through a questionnaire distributed to every member of Congress via the offices of Representative Jeffrey Cohelan and Senator Alan Cranston, both of California.[13]

The spirit of this inquiry was clearly conveyed in the preface to von Hippel and Primack's report. In discussing the role of senior scientists who have served as technical advisers to the government, the two physicists wrote the following:

> Their efforts are mainly dedicated to the service of the Executive Branch of the federal government, and almost all of their advice is secret. We are concerned that the confidentiality of this advice may undermine essential democratic controls on the direction of technology, while at the same time weakening the force of the technical advice itself by depriving it of a visible constituency. We find it difficult to escape the conclusion that the "insider" approach of the "pros" who comprise the advisory establishment of the Executive Branch needs to be complemented by a more open advisory system for Congress and the public. The technical community has a great responsibility to educate and lead the nation in the constructive development and application of technology.[14]

The problem, von Hippel and Primack argued, was that Congress lacked sufficient "independent sources of scientific and technical advice" and, as a result, operated at a disadvantage to the executive branch, which had at its command vast reservoirs of technical experts, information, and money. They observed:

> Technical personnel who appear before Congress are often tainted, in Congressional eyes, by close association with the Executive. Frequently they are advocates of legislation or funding for projects desired by a federal agency or a special interest. Such witnesses may engage in selective disclosure of information or otherwise try to mislead Congress. Other scientific testimony may actually be value judgments in disguise—a disguise Congressmen are fortunately increasingly able to penetrate. Still other scientific information is in fact misinformation, delivered by scientists speaking in areas different from those in which they

acquired their prestige. It is difficult for even the sharpest and best informed Congressman to sort out good from bad technical advice and information; partly as a result, even the most costly Administration technical programs are frequently evaluated by Congress on political and other non-technical grounds.[15]

The task force's recommendations were not all original, as with its endorsement of creating a Congressional Office of Technology Assessment, an idea that had been widely debated for several years.[16] Nevertheless, it did advance one proposal that had received little previous attention: establishment of a congressional intern program for young scientists and engineers. These interns, von Hippel and Primack said, would be selected through a national competition and would spend a year with a congressional member or committee "with special responsibilities in technical areas." They added that "the continual infusion of new blood would tend to stimulate the permanent staff. We think also that the effect of bringing young researchers into contact with the Congressional process could quickly make an important contribution in helping the technical community come to grips with the problems facing our society."[17]

The Stanford workshop posed a range of questions to every member of Congress about scientific and technical advice to the legislative branch as a whole and about the merits of the proposed scientist/engineer intern program in particular. Of the 73 respondents (62 representatives and 11 senators), 18 members said that they liked the idea of a scientist/engineer intern program as a way of improving the available technical advice, while four members opposed the idea.[18] In summarizing the responses, von Hippel and Primack reported that the intern program was one of the workshop's most popular proposals, although it raised a few negative remarks as well. "Written comments ranged from 'This has merit. Good idea' to 'Hell no! No Longhairs,'" they said, concluding that "this is probably the type of action which could be decided on by individual Congressmen and committees."[19]

American Association for the Advancement of Science

Of all the workshop participants, Primack remained the most outspoken advocate for placing young scientists and engineers on the staffs of congressional offices. After receiving his doctorate in 1970, he accepted an appointment as a junior Fellow at Harvard University, and from that post he persistently lobbied the American Physical Society (APS) and the American Association for the Advancement of Science to develop a fellowship program. He gained the ear of the AAAS leadership through his appointment as a nonvoting, junior member of the association's Committee on Science in the Promotion of Human Welfare.[20] As such, Primack joined a select group of young researchers who served as spokespersons for the new generation of scientists caught up in the social ferment of the 1960s.

In the wake of ad hoc workshops, protests, and general disruptions that had punctuated several of the association's annual meetings in the late 1960s, the AAAS board of directors had expressed its approval that the scientific community become more socially relevant, declaring in 1969 that the association should dedicate itself to increasing the "effectiveness of its work on the chief contemporary problems concerning the mutual relations of science, technology, and social change."[21] The board had also decided on a self-imposed reform: beginning with its December 1969 meeting, each board member was to bring along a young colleague who would be allowed to participate in the board's opening day of deliberations, thus exposing the association's elders to the needs, aspirations, and concerns of the nation's younger researchers. When the board met privately in executive session on the second day, however, the junior guests convened their own private meeting, where they drafted a recommendation that called upon AAAS to formalize this experiment by creating a permanent Committee of Young Scientists (COYS), with each COYS member to be assigned a seat on one of the association's standing committees. The board concurred, implementing all the recommendations with the exception of establishing COYS as a permanent committee. Rather, it was established on an ad hoc basis and its name was later changed to the AAAS Youth Council.[22]

Primack was appointed to the Youth Council in 1970, and he used that new-found platform to advance the congressional fellowship idea. In its March 1970 report to the AAAS board of directors, the Youth Council recommended the creation of a scientist internship exchange program that would place young scientists within government agencies at the federal, state, and local levels, where they would lend their technical competence to relevant issues for a period of one year. The council's notion was that the interns would return to their academic positions after the year of service, so that the "internship would broaden but not destroy their scientific careers."[23]

Discussion of a science and technology internship program took place within the larger context of serious debate about the need for better informed congressional decision making, which included a capability for technology assessment within the legislative branch. In April 1971, for example, Connecticut Representative Emilio Q. Daddario spoke before the AAAS Committee on Science in the Promotion of Human Welfare about the "development of an early-warning system so that the Congress could develop a legislative capability of policy determination in applied science and technology that would be both anticipatory and adaptive rather than reactionary and symptomatic." Daddario claimed that his colleagues were developing an increased awareness of their need for technology assessments, but that the scientific community did not as a whole understand the needs of the legislative branch. Scientists and engineers, he said, knew the executive branch far better, having had long experience working for various agencies, which had the funds to pay for their services. Daddario called on AAAS and the scientific community in general to increase their interplay with Congress.[24]

The concept of scientist-interns continued to occupy Primack's thinking, and in September 1971 he wrote AAAS board member Richard H. Bolt about the refined idea of limiting such a program to a "Congressional internship for scientists." As with the earlier proposal, the program would be directed toward scientists in the early stages of their careers. The benefits to Congress, Primack argued, would be many: "bright young people with technical training strengthening staff capability, particularly in evaluation of technological proposals and scientific testimony." Beyond the internship year, he envisioned some of the scientist-interns choosing to remain in public service, thus adding permanently to the professional staff of Congress. On the other hand, he wrote, "the scientist-intern would have an opportunity to learn how government really works, knowledge that cannot fail to come in handy in later work whether in universities, industry, or government."[25]

There would be trade-offs, he told Bolt. "The disadvantage to the scientist primarily interested in research," he said, "would be a postponement or interruption of his career. Of course, the current unfortunate shortage of jobs might make the internship more attractive even to researchers." Primack suggested that the scientist internship program might be folded in with the American Political Science Association's already well-established congressional fellowship program. By way of background, he told Bolt that he had "explored the question of the American Physical Society sponsoring one or more Congressional interns. The treasurer, Joe Burton, thought this a possibly practicable idea, and so did APS President Ed Purcell." Although nothing had yet materialized from these discussions, Primack thought AAAS might be able to count on APS—and probably other scientific societies—to recruit and fund interns for an overall program administered by AAAS. "I am under no illusions that a Congressional intern program for scientists would solve any currently pressing problems," Primack said in closing. "But it would help Congress, and it also would help the technical community come to grips with the serious imbalance existing between Congress and the Executive Branch in their capacity to analyze and influence national technological policy."[26]

The Committee on Science in the Promotion of Human Welfare embraced Primack's clearly articulated ideas and framework. Following up Primack's letter to Bolt, which the latter introduced to this committee along with the 1970 Youth Council report, the committee paraphrased the young physicist's language in crafting its own appeal to the AAAS's board of directors to initiate an "AAAS Program of Government Internships for Scientists." It argued that such a program had been "proposed to the AAAS through formal and informal channels" and that "such internships, appropriately structured, could make practical contributions to the effective use of scientific knowledge in government and to the training of persons for careers involving public uses of scientific information." Moreover, the committee contended, "the operation of such internships would appear to be relevant to the fulfillment of AAAS objectives."[27]

The recommendation was greeted with great favor at the board of directors' October 1971 meeting. The board instructed the association's staff to explore sources of extramural funding for the scientist internship program. AAAS's Executive Officer William Bevan placed Director of Science and Society Programs Richard Scribner in charge of the effort.[28]

By January 1972, Scribner had compiled a list of key questions related to the potential "scientist intern program." These issues included whether or not the recipient organization (say a congressional committee or an individual member's office) should be required to pay a portion of the intern's salary. Arguments in favor of so doing were a reduction in the program's cost to AAAS and the possibility of enhancing the intern's value to the recipient organization, because the congressional office would be allocating its own resources to that person.[29] Noting that the American Political Science Association fellowship program granted its Fellows great latitude in determining their congressional placements, the AAAS staff debated the degree of freedom they should offer their own interns in choosing assignments. AAAS staff probed how best to orient and brief the scientist-interns and how to anticipate the likely growth and impact of the program. In selecting interns from the applicant pool, the staff weighed the pros and cons of including representatives from the recipient organizations on the selection committee. Finally, staff questioned the rhetorical implications of the term "intern," which was widely used to identify the hundreds of high school and college students temporarily assisting Congress.[30] Following the practice of the political scientists, they soon turned to the term "Fellow."

These notions were fleshed out in a subsequent internal document. Again, the proposed program was broadly conceived and projected AAAS's placing young (ages 23 to 35) scientists and engineers with Congress *and* with federal, state, and local government offices. Like any fellowship program, the report stated, "this one is based upon the premise, supported by a long tradition in American education, that learning in the formal structured classroom can be usefully supplemented by practical field experience." According to the staff report, AAAS was wholly justified in engaging in this enterprise because of its stature as "the oldest and largest major general scientific organization in the United States and the world's largest federation of scientific and engineering societies."[31]

The staff report offered the following rationale for the proposed program: "(1) provide the opportunity for young scientists and engineers to spend a year working at the interface of science and technology with policy making or policy implementation, (2) broaden the perspective of both the scientific communities and the governmental communities regarding the value of such scientific-government interaction and emphasizing such service at all levels of government, (3) enable the recruitment of some of the interns for permanent positions." The benefits of such a program were said to be many. Congress, for example, would benefit from "the strengthening of staff capability by the addition, where needed, of people with scientific and technical training; for example, strengthening capability in the early consideration of the scientific or technological aspects of an issue under study, in the evaluation of technological proposals and scientific testimony, and in the inclusion of reasonable scientific statements or requirements in legislation under preparation."[32]

The report highlighted what the scientific community could expect to reap through the establishment of the program: "(a) the opening of a new non-classroom education experience for those chosen to be interns; (b) the impact of this experience on the students, faculty, and programs after the return of some of the interns to teaching positions; (c) the building of new links between scientific and engineering communities and governmental groups; (d) the development of a way for some younger, less established, but nonetheless competent scientists to contribute to government; and (e) the increased understanding of government processes of those interns who return to academic positions and national laboratories."[33]

The staff report was not so naive as to suggest that the fellowship program would solve any of society's problems, but it did insist that it could contribute to the government's ability to deal with them. "It may also help the technical and governmental communities find ways to correct the imbalance existing between Congress and the Executive Branch in their respective capacities to analyze and influence national scientific and technological policy," the report claimed. It would accomplish that, in part, by expanding the scientific and engineering talent available to congressional staffs. Speaking more parochially, the report stated that "such a program cannot be expected to alleviate the unemployment problem of scientists and engineers, but it will demonstrate the existence of non-traditional careers in government service..."[34] This disparity came not so much from the inability of Congress to obtain technical advice—it already received a superabundance of such information from the executive branch agencies, from lobbyists, and from the hearings it orchestrated—but from the difficulty it had in *evaluating* that advice. This problem was especially true when experts disagreed about a particular scientific or technical matter. The Fellows were meant to mediate this gap—to help evaluate and to translate.[35]

Recruitment and selection of the association's Fellows would be handled entirely by AAAS, but the staff recommended that the placements be determined entirely on the basis of "mutual acceptability" between the host office and the individual Fellow "through the mechanism of an interview."[36]

Early in the establishment of the Congressional Science and Engineering Fellows Program, the AAAS leadership decided that it would not select, sponsor, and reimburse all of the Fellows, but instead would serve as an umbrella operation for Fellows supported by its sister societies. The association would raise funds for a small number of its own Fellows, but the bulk of the program would rely on efforts of other professional organizations, who would pay a management fee to AAAS for each participant in the program.[37] Proselytizing thus became one of the early missions, as AAAS sought to get other scientific and engineering societies to see the advantages of and opportunities (and responsibility) for banding together and establishing an ongoing program to introduce technically trained people into staff positions on Capitol Hill.

Scribner began meeting with sympathetic members of Congress early in the process to assess the perceived need for scientists and engineers as staff members and—most important—to identify potential receiving offices for the "Visiting Scientist in Congress" program.[38] Although Scribner used this title in early 1972, the congressional placements comprised but one arm of the intended fellowship program. Other placements would also situate Fellows with state and local government offices, as well as with federal agencies. As Scribner stated in his communications to congressional members: "Besides the important educational purpose, the program should also make significant practical contributions to the more effective use of scientific knowledge in government, broaden the perspective of both the scientific and government communities regarding the value of such service at all levels of government, and contribute to the training and recruitment of persons for careers involving public use of scientific and technical information." To differentiate the AAAS effort from that of the American Political Science Association program, he added that "the service to government aspect is given more weight in our proposed program than in a comparable shorter-term participant-observer fellowship program."[39]

Scribner's efforts to advance the science and engineering fellowship program were sidetracked in spring 1972, when he was reassigned to organize the association's forthcoming December meeting. The AAAS Youth Council, which held the Fellows program as one of its highest priorities, became impatient with this delay. Joel Primack, in particular, tenaciously pursued the fellowship proposal and periodically prodded Scribner to shift his priorities toward implementing the program.[40]

American Society of Mechanical Engineers

The hiatus in AAAS's establishment of a congressional fellowship program cost the association its chance to become the first scientific/engineering society to provide the legislative branch with a formal source of technically trained staff assistance. That distinction was achieved by the American Society of Mechanical Engineers (ASME), which quietly began its own modest congressional fellowship program in August 1972, with its first Fellow on the job in January 1973.

Like most scientific and engineering societies at the time, ASME found itself under internal and external pressure to address more actively the major social problems confronting the United States. In 1971, for example, the mechanical engineers adopted an "Overriding Goal" that called upon ASME "to move vigorously from what is now a society with essentially technical concerns to a society that, while serving the technical interests of its members ever better, is increasingly professional in its outlook, sensitive to the engineer's responsibility to the public's interest, and dedicated to a leadership role in making technology a true servant of man."[41] When Washington Representative Mike McCormack sent out letters in October 1971 to several professional societies soliciting their help with the newly formed Committee on Science and Astronautics Task Force on Energy, which he headed, ASME became one of the few organizations to respond enthusiastically. Hoping to explore ways in which the society might realize its overriding goal through interacting with the task force, the ASME executive committee arranged a meeting with McCormack in December. Immediately preceding that encounter, McCormack huddled with his task force staff—J. Thomas Ratchford and John Andelin (perhaps the only two Ph.D. physicists then working as congressional staff)[42]—to discuss what he might ask of the mechanical engineers. The three men decided to request two actions from ASME: (1) that it establish an office in Washington, D.C., where the society's congressional liaison would be easily accessible; and (2) that it sponsor engineering Fellows who would work on Capitol Hill.[43]

Bolstered by the confidence that there was something tangible they could do to assist Congress, ASME executives wasted little time in following through with McCormack's first suggestion: in early 1972, the mechanical engineers established a new office in Washington and hired their first congressional liaison, William P. Miller, Jr. They were a bit more cautious when it came to starting a fellowship program. Before asking their membership to support such an enterprise, they sent Miller to question members of Congress and their staffs about the practicality of such a program. In particular, they sought the advice of the few technically trained staff then working for the legislative branch.[44] In July, Miller summarized what various congressional staff members had advised him regarding "desirable qualifications" for engineering Fellows. "We should seek a man from industry or a man from the Academic Community with some industry experience," Miller told his colleagues. "If possible, a Ph.D. with some broad M.E. background, not tied too tightly to one specialty. He should in addition possess the following qualities: (1) Broad outlook; (2) Good communicator (written and oral); (3) Work well with people; (4) Willing to learn; (5) Not sensitive; (6) Neat appearance; (7) Has some desire for future involvement in some level of government."[45]

Following the sanction by the executive committee of the ASME council, the mechanical engineers announced the establishment of a congressional fellowship program in August 1972. The society would pay half the Fellows' stipend, while the employers of the Fellows would pay the other half. Employers would grant their employees a sabbatical year off with the understanding that the Fellows would later resume their employment. According to the society, "the program is seen as a step toward better technical input in the setting of public policy."[46] When Joel Primack inquired about ASME's plans as part of his fact-finding mission for AAAS, ASME Assistant Executive Director E.H. Walton explained that "we consider the selection of a single person for this post this year to be in the nature of a trial and have not at this point established firm rules for the selection process or predetermined conditions for the year of service." Walton said that the experimental nature of the program led the mechanical engineers to avoid giving the program wide publicity. He emphasized the importance of the American Political Science Association model, but given their different objectives, the mechanical engineers decided to go it on their own. He welcomed AAAS's interest, however, and offered his society's help.[47]

Aside from this brief interaction, ASME struck out independently with its own congressional fellowship program, with no consultation with APS or AAAS staff members. Although it lacked a formal orientation program or a high visibility search, the society placed its first Fellow, Barry I. Hyman, in January 1973. Hyman, who earned his doctorate in engineering mechanics from Virginia Polytechnic Institute in 1965, came to the ASME fellowship as an associate professor in George Washington University's department of civil, mechanical, and environmental engineering. He took a position with the Senate Committee on Commerce, Science, and Transportation, where he worked on such issues as reduction of energy waste and the improvement of automobile fuel economy. Halfway through his fellowship year, Hyman conveyed his impressions of the new program to the engineering community. He explained the wide range of executive branch programs and proposals that embodied complex technological aspects, all of which placed Congress "under a severe handicap" when it came time to assess their merits and establish relevant policy positions. "In spite of this obvious need for engineering expertise," he said, "the generally prevalent image of the engineer as an industry spokesman rather than as an independent professional is responsible for a general reluctance to better utilize individual engineers and the engineering professional societies in advisory capacities." Hyman was confident that the new ASME fellowship program would help improve this situation by "establishing within Congress a new sense of respect for the engineering profession and a consequent willingness to seek its advice more frequently. The natural result of such a development would be a greatly enhanced public image of the engineering profession as being dedicated to using technology for the public good."[48]

The Multiple-Society Effort

While ASME actions made evident the realistic nature of a congressional science and engineering fellowship program, and although the rationale for such an enterprise had gained clarity and momentum throughout 1972, it eluded implementation until 1973, when AAAS Treasurer William T. Golden argued successfully with his fellow members of the board of directors and persuaded them to move forward by providing the necessary seed money through an anonymous personal gift. Golden had become committed to at least testing the viability of an AAAS congressional Fellows program at the association's December 1972 meeting, following his attendance at an AAAS Youth Council meeting.[49] Golden had asked council member Primack to estimate the cost of establishing a fellowship program. Primack reported that expenses would probably run less than $20,000 per Fellow per year, including administrative expenses. The prospect of creating a mechanism that would infuse scientists and engineers into congressional staffs had an irresistible appeal to Golden, who had championed the establishment of the presidential science advisory apparatus in 1951, and that winter he agreed to underwrite two AAAS Fellows on a trial basis.[50]

Golden's philosophy was simple. He believed three elements were necessary for the fellowship program to succeed: money, congressional offices willing to host the Fellows, and qualified scientists and engineers willing to serve as Fellows. Golden's gift satisfied the first need. He now challenged the Youth Council and the AAAS staff to see if the two other needs could also be met. "There is little sense in going to a congressman on a theoretical basis," he advised (something that Scribner had already been doing). Congressional members had to be convinced that a supply of potential Fellows existed. To do that, Golden tried to persuade Primack and other members of the Youth Council to locate qualified young scientists who expressed a willingness to serve as Fellows. Primack initially begged off, claiming he was too busy and that he was hesitant to employ the "buddy system" in nominating Fellows. Golden disagreed with him on the latter point, at least for the launching of the program. He recommended that the Youth Council recruit people in whom they had "personal confidence." Being exceedingly pragmatic, Golden believed the program's success would hinge on the quality of the first Fellows, thus, in his mind, justifying a targeted, personalized search that first year.[51]

The Youth Council, which had been urging AAAS to institute a congressional fellowship program for months, now found itself—thanks to Golden—in a position to tangibly influence events. As Golden told council Chairman William Drayton, if the council members could produce a list of qualified and interested Fellows, then he could assure that the money would be in place and that the AAAS staff would canvass Congress to identify offices willing to host the science and engineering Fellows. Drayton acted immediately, distributing a memorandum to all council members asking that they forward their nominations to Primack. "For obvious reasons," he added, "these first two interns must be first rate."[52] Primack had agreed to head the informal search, and by spring he had forwarded a list of potential Fellows to Golden and AAAS.[53]

With funding secured for its own Fellows and a list of potential candidates in hand, AAAS officials called a meeting with their counterparts in the American Physical Society (APS) and Institute of Electrical and Electronics Engineers (IEEE) to ask if they were ready and willing to form a cooperative fellowship program that would start in the fall. The timing seemed right, and they unanimously agreed to move forward.[54] Beginning with these three professional societies, and joined permanently or temporarily by nearly 40 others during the next two decades, whatever success the congressional fellowship program enjoyed resulted from the continual willingness of the various organizations to work together.

AAAS announced its new fellowship in the 13 April 1973 issue of *Science* magazine in an editorial written by Richard Scribner. Scribner stressed that the overall initiative involved several scientific and engineering societies, and that together they hoped to attract others to join the effort in the years to come. The participating societies were not "promulgating the erroneous philosophy that 'only science can save the world,'" he insisted, but added that "science and technology are crucial elements in the consideration of many problems facing decision makers." He continued:

> The congressional staff includes a few people with strong scientific or engineering backgrounds, but the resources available to congressmen for informing themselves about the technical components of national issues and effectively utilizing existing scientific information are considerably less than those available to the Executive Branch. The reorganized Congressional Research Service and the emerging Office of Technology Assessment will provide greater informational resources, but the utilization of these by individual congressmen often requires an in-office capability.[55]

The rationale for sustaining a science and engineering fellowship program was refined over time as the participating societies prepared funding proposals, which forced their staffs to articulate the main purposes of the program. In seeking financial support from the Charles F. Kettering Foundation in January 1973,

AAAS Executive Officer William Bevan, Jr., stated: "Benefits to the Congress will include the strengthening of staff capability in an area where it is acknowledged to be weak and the development of a corps of individuals of proven capability in government service with strong scientific credentials who can be directly recruited for permanent and responsible staff positions."[56] By June, Scribner applied for a small grant from the Milbank Memorial Fund, claiming that among the program's purposes was "developing new career options for younger scientists" and "further encouraging science policy as an area of study for the natural scientific community."[57] Bevan later pushed a similar theme in seeking support from the Russell Sage Foundation. Aside from the program's use in opening new career paths for social scientists, natural scientists, and engineers, Bevan emphasized the priority to be placed upon "the concept of the public service role for scientists."[58]

Following the program's first year, William Golden pointed to the Fellows' contributions in helping to "bridge the 'two-culture gap.'" As befitted his public and private life, Golden also persistently underscored the need "to increase the involvement of the scientific community in such public service activities."[59] When the Optical Society of America made appeals to its membership to support a congressional fellowship program, it listed as the first rationale the creation of "a new public service opportunity for younger, Ph.D.-level engineers and scientists." Moreover, it argued that "when the Fellows return to their regular jobs, they will bring to the scientific community a new kind of understanding of government."[60]

Members of the scientific establishment seeking to create a new mechanism to provide science and engineering staff assistance to Congress were not working in a vacuum. They were, in fact, keenly aware of the congressional fellowship program that had been run successfully by the American Political Science Association (APSA) for some 20 years. APSA, which was formed in 1903, initiated the congressional fellowships as part of its 50th anniversary celebration. The program sought to focus more scholarly attention on the legislative branch of government and to enhance public understanding of Congress, thereby promoting better government.[61]

American Political Science Association

From the start, the APSA congressional fellowship program brought both political scientists and journalists to Capitol Hill for a 10-month stint.[62] The fellowship started in the fall with a four-week orientation, after which the Fellows divided their remaining nine months between one assignment in the House of Representatives and another in the Senate.[63] Fellows, who were encouraged to split their assignments between an individual member's staff and a committee or subcommittee staff, were responsible for negotiating their individual placements. APSA staff assisted by identifying congressional offices interested in hosting a Fellow. The association's Fellows came at no cost to the congressional offices where they worked; Fellows' stipends were covered either by grants to APSA or through support from their previous employers. Beginning in the early 1950s with six Fellows per year, 20 years later the political scientists were administering a program averaging more than 40 Fellows per year.[64]

Although the APSA fellowship program was primarily oriented toward political scientists and journalists, its subset of Fellows from the executive branch of government occasionally brought in a technically trained civil servant to serve as a congressional Fellow. J. Thomas Ratchford, who had worked as a physicist with the Air Force Office of Scientific Research before he became an APSA Fellow in 1968-69, was a case in point.[65] A more singular example followed in the enthusiastic light of the first Earth Day in 1970, when the Citizens for Ecological Action at Cornell University sponsored an environmental scientist to work in a congressional office, and contracted to include its "Earth Day Fellow," Walter Westman, in the APSA program.[66]

The architects of the Congressional Science and Engineering Fellowship Program also had the option of affiliating with the political scientists' well-established and respected program. They were ultimately dissuaded, however, by the predominance of professionals already attuned to government and politics. Engineers and scientists, they reasoned, would need a different type of orientation. Moreover, the placement of technically trained professionals (an unusual concept then) seemed to require a tailored promotional effort. AAAS, APS, and IEEE staffs therefore looked closely at the APSA program, hoping to emulate what seemed appropriate to their objectives and to modify what did not. In addition to interviewing APSA staff and former Fellows, the three organizations obtained a copy of Ronald Hedlund's unpublished 1971 report to APSA, "Participant Observation in Studying Congress: The Congressional Fellowship Program," which provided a detailed and critical evaluation of the program's first two decades.[67]

Using the APSA program as their model, the engineering and scientific societies began conceiving their own independent congressional fellowship program. In many respects, the process of recruitment, orientation, individualized placement, and external funding of Fellows mirrored that of the political scientists' program. The differences—aside from emphasis on subject and policy areas—rested mainly in the following: orientation was half as long (two weeks instead of four); the fellowship year lasted 12 months instead of 10; and the Fellows were to work the entire period for a single congressional office (instead of splitting their assignments between the House and Senate).[68] It was this latter point—duration of service—that scientists and engineers most heavily emphasized when distinguishing their program from that of the political scientists. The APSA program divided the fellowship assignments to maximize the educational benefits for its Fellows. The Congressional Science and Engineering Fellowship Program, however, placed its greatest emphasis on serving Congress. As AAAS's Arthur Purcell stated in the association's press release, by placing Fellows with a single congressional office for an entire year, "we hope to present a greater opportunity for utilization of a fellow's talents; hence, the AAAS Scientist-Fellowship Program has a greater service-to-government component."[69]

CHAPTER 2

Launching the Joint Fellowship Program

With funding in hand for only a single year, the Congressional Science and Engineering Fellowship Program had to produce positive results if it hoped to extend to a second or third season. Promoters of the fellowship idea were keenly aware of the experimental nature of the enterprise and that its success or failure depended a great deal on how Congress received the first class of Fellows. Even with positive experiences, the participating societies faced the challenge of securing long-term funding. Moreover, to succeed they needed to attract top quality applicants year in and year out, while expanding the number of sister scientific and engineering societies willing to join with them in the AAAS-administered program. Ultimately, however, the litmus test was Congress itself: Did the members and their staffs find the science and engineering Fellows sufficiently valuable that they would offer them positions year after year? In short, did the Fellows program meet the needs of Congress?

While the latter test would have to await the performance of the various Fellows, AAAS staff tackled the more practical and immediate challenge of obtaining a stable source of funding (initially aimed at a three-year block). As Richard A. Scribner and Arthur H. Purcell noted in their first progress report, the fellowship program should be viewed as "a pilot program to demonstrate [especially to the major philanthropic foundations] the feasibility and viability of our approach."[1]

When the AAAS staff tested the waters of the potential pool of fellowship applicants in the spring of 1973, staff were delighted at the response: 90 applications came across the transom within the 45-day opening period. Equally important, applicants came from diverse employment situations, including academic, industrial, and government positions; diverse geographic locations; and diverse disciplinary backgrounds (physicists led all other groups with 27 applications, while chemists represented the second largest pool with 18).[2]

The response from Congress was also encouraging: 47 representatives, 23 senators, and 10 committees expressed their interest in hosting a Fellow. The 80 respondents listed several legislative initiatives for which they most desired technical assistance, but energy and environment were far and away the most frequently cited areas of interest.[3] For example, Washington Senator Henry M. Jackson wrote that "such a fellowship program for scientists and engineers would provide a valuable assist to Congressional committees and to members alike as we are faced with many technical and complex scientific questions involved in the legislative program before the Congress." Jackson, chairman of the Interior and Insular Affairs Committee, added that he did "not have to emphasize the importance of the problems facing the Nation with respect to our fuels and energy supply." His hope was to find a technically trained Fellow willing to work with his staff in the development of legislation to "provide a crash program for research and development of the energy technology to help make the Nation self-sufficient in the years ahead."[4]

The operation of the fellowship program that first year established the basic framework that was to change little during the next two decades. In the spring of that year, AAAS staff sent letters to every congressional member describing the program and soliciting expressions of interest on their behalf, along with indications of the issues with which they expected to be working during the upcoming year. Positive responses were then compiled into a portfolio of "openings," which Fellows were encouraged to consult in the fall, following the conclusion of their orientation.[5]

Settling on the formal name of the program was not as simple as one might expect. By calling it the AAAS Congressional

Fellowship Program in its initial recruitment literature, AAAS prompted the American Political Science Association (APSA) administrative officials to call repeatedly for a name change, arguing that APSA had a proprietary claim on the terminology "Congressional Fellowship Program."[6] When AAAS turned to titles such as "AAAS Congressional Scientist-Fellow Program" or "AAAS Congressional Scientist Fellows Program," the APSA staff remained concerned that Congress and the broader public might still confuse the AAAS program with the APSA Congressional Fellowship Program. As APSA Assistant Director Walter E. Beach wrote in October 1973: "We feel that this name [AAAS Congressional Scientist Fellows] will be shortened by many to Congressional Fellows and as such be confused with our group. As I indicated to you, we prefer something which does not put the word Congressional before the word Fellow, i.e., AAAS Science Fellows in Congress."[7] By 1974, AAAS stuck with the title Congressional Science and Engineering Fellowship Program despite protests of the political scientists.

The First Class of Fellows

Scribner recalled how he and the first class of Fellows essentially "flew by the seats of our pants" during the program's inaugural year, as there were no truly relevant models to follow, little or no experience on the part of congressional members in working with scientists and engineers, and a wide and disparate set of expectations for what the Fellows could and should do. Also, the program's participants were aware of the extent to which the continuation and future direction of the fellowship program depended upon their performance. These circumstances generated a sense of adventure and worked to create a strong sense of comradeship among that initial cohort of Fellows.[8]

Four of the six Fellows worked on energy-related issues, which conformed to the findings of the congressional responses to the questionnaire distributed earlier in 1973. All six Fellows found satisfactory placements, which are summarized below.[9]

Benjamin S. Cooper was a 31-year-old assistant professor of physics at Iowa State University who had earned his physics Ph.D.

from the University of Virginia in 1968. In addition to his academic responsibilities, Cooper involved himself with the Iowa Democratic Party and served as a 1972 state convention delegate. As an American Physical Society (APS) Congressional Fellow, he worked for the Senate Interior and Insular Affairs Committee,[10] where he assisted the energy policy staff. Although soon spurred by the oil embargo, the Senate staff had already become increasingly engaged with energy-related issues. In May 1971, for example, the Senate established the National Fuels and Energy Policy Study as a means to foster cooperation among the Interior Committee, the Public Works Committee, the Commerce Committee, and the Joint Committee on Atomic Energy. As a physicist, Cooper was asked to participate in this umbrella study group by serving as a liaison between the Interior Committee and the Joint Committee. Cooper's most substantive, long-term effort came with his involvement with the Energy Information Act, which sought to make available timely and accurate energy-related statistical information. Such information was wanted immediately, as the Congress and the executive branch sought to assess the likely impact of the Arab oil embargo on the availability of petroleum within the U.S.[11]

N. Richard Werthamer was a physicist from Bell Laboratories and was selected as the second APS Fellow. He spent his fellowship year working for the personal office of Ohio Representative Charles A. Mosher, who was involved in a number of science-related activities. Such activities stemmed from Mosher's positions as ranking minority member of the House Committee on Science and Astronautics and ranking minority member of the House Committee on Merchant Marine and Fisheries' Subcommittee on Oceanography. Following Werthamer's appointment to Mosher's office, Mosher was selected as vice chairman of the Technology Assessment Board of the Office of Technology Assessment (OTA). Werthamer assisted the congressman with various duties associated with a personal office; for example, responding to constituent inquiries and assisting with the preparation of speeches. Werthamer also helped with Mosher's committee responsibilities, especially those of the Energy Subcommittee, where Werthamer organized a hearing on wind power. For OTA, he did background research on an assessment of outer continental shelf petroleum production.[12]

Michael L. Telson was a 27-year-old electrical engineer who had earned four degrees in electrical engineering from Massachusetts Institute of Technology (MIT): a B.S. in 1967, an M.S. in 1969, an E.E. in 1971, and a Ph.D. in 1973. He had consulted with environmental public interest groups on issues related to energy economics and the environment. Also, he had worked one summer as a management analyst for New York City's Bureau of the Budget. He was selected as an AAAS Fellow. Like Cooper, Telson worked for the Senate Committee on Interior and Insular Affairs, concentrating on energy issues such as legislation related to the Nonnuclear Energy R&D Act, the law establishing the Federal Energy Administration and the Energy Research and Development Administration, and more general congressional probes into oil pricing and the energy policy implications of the financial stability of the U.S. electric utility industry.

Elliot A. Segal was a 35-year-old assistant dean at the Yale University School of Medicine. He was a public health specialist who had received two master's degrees from Yale in 1965: one in public health and one in urban studies. Segal had worked as both a consultant and a volunteer for various local and state health services associations. He served as one of the AAAS congressional Fellows, accepting a placement with Washington Senator Warren Magnuson.

Jessica Tuchman was a 27-year-old biologist who received her bachelor of arts from Radcliffe College in 1967 and her Ph.D. in biochemistry and biophysics from California Institute of Technology in 1973. She had volunteered as a staff worker for the McCarthy for President Committee. Tuchman joined Telson and Segal as an AAAS Fellow. Her assignment was with the personal staff of Arizona Representative Morris Udall, assisting his work on the Subcommittee on the Environment (Committee on Interior and Insular Affairs), including drafting major energy legislation.[13]

Ronal W. Larson, an electrical engineer at Georgia Institute of Technology, was sponsored by the Institute of Electrical and Electronics Engineers. He spent his fellowship year working simultaneously for two subcommittees of the House Committee on

Science and Astronautics: the Energy Subcommittee (chaired by Mike McCormack) and the Science, Research and Development Subcommittee (chaired by John Davis). Larson assisted the subcommittees with a variety of energy-related issues, although his principal contribution was in solar energy legislation.

Although not formally a participant in the collaborative program, American Society of Mechanical Engineers (ASME) Fellow Barry Hyman was invited by Richard Scribner to participate in the Fellows' social and intellectual group activities. Hyman had started his independent fellowship eight months earlier than the other Fellows. Despite Hyman's satisfactory assignment with the Senate Commerce Committee, he had experienced a deep sense of professional isolation, being the sole engineering Fellow on Capitol Hill, without the social and professional support structure enjoyed by either the American Political Science Association Fellows or the science and engineering Fellows.[14]

Scribner repeatedly solicited ASME's official participation in the science and engineering fellowship program.[15] Despite parallel efforts within ASME and AAAS, mechanical engineering Fellows participated only informally in the AAAS-administered program. As Scribner told the engineers in February 1976, because AAAS had been inviting past ASME Fellows to join in their various programs from the beginning, a formalized relationship would be more than welcomed. "I would hope that, in view of the substantial effort and associated cost," he said, "ASME would see fit to contribute, in appropriate fashion, to defraying some of these program costs. A symbolic contribution at this point might be all that is needed to cement the relationship."[16] The ASME leadership appreciated AAAS's overtures and agreed to establish formal ties with the collaborative enterprise in fall 1976.[17]

Energy and Environmental Policy Concerns

The first class of Fellows proved to be valued members of Capitol Hill, indicated by the fact that all six of them were offered congressional staff positions at the close of their fellowships. Five ultimately accepted.[18] The specific nature of their contributions to

Congress was significantly influenced by two major trends of the day: environmentalism and the energy crisis. Both issues lent themselves to involvement by technically trained individuals. This involvement helped to create a receptive climate for the new science and engineering fellowship program and to ensure a mutually satisfactory relationship among host offices and their Fellows. As Henry M. Jackson wrote in June 1974: "The Committee is pleased with the program and with the performance of Dr. Michael Telson and Dr. Benjamin Cooper who have made a significant contribution to the work of the Committee in connection with our ongoing Fuels and Energy Study."[19]

In particular, the energy crisis was instrumental in prefiguring assignments offered to (and accepted by) many of the first science and engineering Fellows. The crisis was precipitated in November 1973 when the Arabs curtailed oil exports to the United States because of U.S. support of Israel in the Middle East war. The three-month oil embargo and the perceived ability of the Organization of Petroleum Exporting Countries (OPEC) to control the price of crude oil resulted in a near panic in the United States, as horror stories of long lines at gasoline stations and rumors of pending fuel rationing filled the headlines of the nation's newspapers. Beyond the personal impact on individual citizens, the country as a whole appeared imperiled, as energy and national security came to be widely seen as indelibly intertwined. The cachet of scientific and engineering expertise rose, as responses to the oil crisis inevitably involved evaluations of technical alternatives. Such alternatives included development of alternative fuel sources, expansion of nuclear power plant construction, shifts in fuel sources by industry, imposition of energy conservation requirements, and encouragement of domestic oil exploration.[20] The need for technical and scientific literacy among their staff led those members of Congress responsible for energy policy to see the advantage of hosting science and engineering Fellows.

Washington Representative Mike McCormack was a case in point. As a freshman congressman, McCormack landed the chairmanship of the newly established Task Force on Energy within the House Committee on Science and Astronautics in July 1971. The task force had little real authority, in that the chairman had no budget with which to operate. Aside from the letterhead, visibility, and appearance of prestige, McCormack had to rely primarily on the assistance of the Congressional Research Service and the part-time help of J. Thomas Ratchford, a physicist and former American Political Science Association Congressional Fellow who had joined the staff of the Subcommittee on Science, Research, and Development. In October, John Andelin, also a physicist, joined McCormack as a $100-per-month staff assistant on the task force.[21] When the House Committee on Science and Astronautics created a new Subcommittee on Energy the following year, McCormack gained the chairmanship, despite his lack of seniority, and he elevated Andelin to a full-salaried staff directorship.[22] McCormack took some pride in encouraging the ASME to launch its congressional engineering fellowship program in 1972. When the Institute of Electrical and Electronics Engineers (IEEE) founded its congressional fellowship program the following year, McCormack shared the services of IEEE Fellow Ronal Larson. Impressed with Larson's contributions, McCormack made known his strong interest in hosting a full-time Fellow during the second year, especially someone with expertise relevant to the field of energy.[23]

Fellows in the following years continued to find opportunities in the areas of energy and the environment, which remained important legislative issues throughout the 1970s and 1980s. Later additions to the fellowship program stressed work in child and health care. The focus of concentration for nearly all of the congressional Fellows differed from the principal topics addressed by science advisors to the White House, where the heaviest use of technical experts came in the realm of military weaponry and national defense.[24] These issues were of prime interest to Congress as well, but because work on these issues required security clearances for staff members—clearances that normally took several months to acquire—it made little sense to use 12-month Fellows for such assignments. Therefore, few Fellows worked on national security matters.[25] Congressional Science and Engineering Fellows thus served in a fundamentally different capacity than scientists and engineers associated with the President's Council of Advisors on Science and Technology (PCAST). As *Science* magazine reporter

Constance Holden explained, the congressional fellowship program cast scientists "not as advisers, but as workers in the political hive."[26]

Regarding concentration on matters relating to energy policy, 1974-75 APS Fellow Allan Hoffman spent the bulk of his year with the Senate Committee on Commerce, Science, and Transportation working on legislation pertaining to automobile fuel economy.[27] Lloyd B. Craine, an IEEE Fellow that same year, also concentrated on energy-related issues during his stint with the House Committee on Science and Technology. Craine's contributions spanned a wide spectrum of policy issues, but revolved primarily around solar energy and fossil fuels.[28]

As the Arab oil crisis renewed congressional interest in energy policy—which in turn created meaningful opportunities for the new science and engineering Fellows—organizational reforms within the federal government added even greater relevance to the fellowship program. The Energy Reorganization Act of 1974 created—in January 1975—two new entities: the Energy Research and Development Administration (ERDA) and the Nuclear Regulatory Commission (NRC). These government agencies consisted of the assembled parts of several long-standing programs, including the Atomic Energy Commission (which was disbanded), the Office of Coal Research, the National Aeronautics and Space Administration, and the National Science Foundation. Three years later, Congress made a corresponding change by abolishing the Joint Committee on Atomic Energy and distributing its responsibilities among several standing committees.[29] President Jimmy Carter, who proclaimed on national television that the effort to address the United States's grave energy problems amounted to "the moral equivalent of war," presented Congress with a procession of energy policy initiatives throughout his administration, which inadvertently helped continue the need for congressional science and engineering Fellows in this area.[30]

In the House of Representatives, the Committee on Science and Technology gained jurisdiction for part of ERDA. In 1975, the committee found itself responsible for much of the agency's authorizing legislation, its proposed budget, the preparation of energy plans, and subsequent oversight of the agency's programs.

The committee responded to the increased demands by reorganizing its subcommittee structure from a single energy subcommittee to two subcommittees: one addressing fossil fuels and another on advanced energy sources.[31] IEEE Fellow Lloyd Craine, who was with the committee at the time, found himself immersed in the issues.[32] Thomas Moss, who worked for the personal office of active committee member George Brown as the 1974-75 APS Fellow, devoted "considerable time" to dealing with energy conservation strategies.[33] Haven Whiteside, Moss's APS colleague that year, said that his fellowship with the Senate Committee on Environment and Public Works' Subcommittee on Environmental Pollution led him to try "to further my own education by learning more about the subjects of environment and energy on which I have been woefully ignorant."[34]

Orientation and Placement

AAAS established its administrative routine right from the start. The fellowship year paralleled that of academe, running from September to August. It began with a two-week orientation in which the new class of Fellows was exposed to the basic institutions and operations of the legislative branch; in short, as Richard Scribner liked to say, it was a crash course in "practical political science."[35] Among the issues addressed were the relations and functions of the three branches of government; how the budget process works; the functions of congressional support agencies (General Accounting Office, Congressional Research Service, Office of Technology Assessment, and Congressional Budget Office); and the relationship of the National Academy of Sciences and the President's Office of Science and Technology Policy to the U.S. Congress.

From the beginning, AAAS sought to engage prominent and experienced speakers for the orientation program, providing new Fellows with a broad spectrum of opinion and perspectives. The Fellows received privileged briefings from members of Congress, congressional staff directors, analysts from the congressional support agencies, executive branch officials, lobbyists, journalists, academics, and other science policy leaders.[36] In addition to introducing the Fellows to how Congress operated, the orientation also sought to give them a better sense of the types of issues likely to be of greatest concern during the forthcoming year. AAAS was consistently able to attract outstanding speakers, which resulted in the orientation's earning a reputation as "the best cram course in science and technology policy available."[37] A secondary consideration—one whose effectiveness no doubt varied tremendously among the different Fellows—was the opportunity to establish professional relationships. Charles Blahous, an American Physical Society congressional Fellow, spoke about this benefit of the orientation. "Mostly, orientation was useful to me because its duration gave sufficient time to establish friendships," he said. "That is its most worthwhile function in my book."[38]

During the third week, the Fellows began interviewing with individual members' offices and committee and subcommittee offices for possible positions. The program encouraged Fellows to find their assignments within two weeks. AAAS staff provided information about which offices and committees were interested in sponsoring Fellows and counseled Fellows on a self-selecting basis, but responsibility for placement remained entirely with the Fellows. Because Fellows were provided to the members and committees with their full salaries paid, there was generally a competition to attract them; typically, each Fellow had two or more opportunities from which to select. Fraternity and sorority members undoubtedly saw similarities between the "rushes" held by their universities' houses, where prospective members and current members sized each other up, and the congressional placement process, where Fellows evaluated the desirability of working with a particular office, and those offices in turn measured their desire to work with the Fellow. In both instances, the ultimate match was based on common attraction. This individualized placement process represented an early AAAS-instituted policy. The policy was meant to avoid the appearance of conflicts of interest that might arise if the professional societies played a role in brokering congressional placements of their Fellows.[39]

The requirement that Fellows secure their own assignments yielded benefits beyond increasing the likelihood of mutually beneficial relationships among Fellows and congressional offices.

Having each year's class interview widely was a form of advertising for the program. Many staff members personally met the scientist and engineer Fellows and learned about the program in the process and what it might offer their office. For the Fellows, the interviewing process, while time-consuming and at times stressful, proved to have an important utility in encouraging each Fellow to extend his or her exposure to Congress, thereby expanding their webs of personal contacts.

The administrative role of the AAAS staff lightened after the three-week orientation and placement period. Thereafter, the staff consulted, monitored, and oversaw the program and its individual participants. To sustain a sense of community among the Fellows and to ensure their continued learning and development of skills (as well as to monitor their progress), AAAS administered a year-long program of seminars.[40] Typically, monthly or bimonthly seminars were associated with a dinner and featured congressional members and staff, journalists, lobbyists, and various analysts or practitioners working within the political process, on science and technology policy, or in both areas. Informal social events also enlivened the fellowship year. As the number of participating societies grew, some of the new organizations chose to convene separate meetings with their Fellows to address more targeted public policy concerns.

Financial Demands

Scribner liked to point to the collegiality promoted by the joint fellowship program. Explaining both the symbolic and practical benefits of banding together, he said that each society "contributes to the management and operations costs associated with running this program, which benefits all of the Fellows and all of the Societies' efforts." However, he hastened to add that "while these contributions accumulate to a significant amount, the lion's share of the associated costs is still borne by the AAAS."[41] The advantages of collaborating extended beyond finances, of course, and went right to the heart of enhancing the visibility and standing of the program. A larger, more diverse fellowship program run in a coordinated, unified manner meant that congressional members and staff would see the effort as more substantial, which would not be evident with several small, independently run efforts.

William T. Golden, AAAS treasurer and member of the board of directors, continued to work behind the scenes to nurture the program, increase its visibility, and solidify a broad base of support for the endeavor within the scientific and engineering communities. For example, in spring 1974, he campaigned to raise private donations for the program, which he described as being "in peril of foundering, for financial reasons." Although AAAS intended to continue administering the program, Golden said the association "has its own financial restraints, which are particularly acute this year, and is not in a position to support the program beyond the provision of certain overhead and other indirect, but real and necessary, administrative costs."[42] Always one who practiced what he preached, Golden himself gave another anonymous gift to the fellowship program that year.[43]

Word of the possibility that AAAS would not fund its own congressional Fellow in 1974 dismayed others besides Golden. For example, Richard Werthamer, an American Physical Society Fellow from the first class, urged Leonard M. Rieser, Jr., chairman of the AAAS board of directors, to reconsider the AAAS's decision not to sponsor its own Fellows, but to rely solely on the two-year Ford Foundation grant (which restricted the three Fellows per year to assignments with the Office of Technology Assessment).[44] This move, Werthamer warned, threatened to "greatly weaken the leadership role that the AAAS has been taking in the congressional fellowship program" and "could ultimately jeopardize the entire program." The former Fellow did not mince words. "I believe," he stated, "that the unwillingness of AAAS to fund even one Fellow from its own internal funds appears to be a denial of the leadership role in this program which it has played so successfully until now. . . . Ultimately the scientists and engineers of the nation must be the ones who support their own involvement, through their societies, in national affairs, and in the legislature particularly. I believe that this support should not only be moral, but should be financial as well, if it is to represent a true commitment."[45]

Despite the efforts of Golden, Werthamer, Scribner, and others, AAAS did not allocate enough internal funds to sponsor independently its own Fellow during the second year. Stipends for all three AAAS Fellows in 1974-75—Henry Kelly, a physicist; Gary Thomas, an electrical engineer; and Jon Veigel, a physical chemist— were financed through a special two-year Ford Foundation grant, which stipulated that all three Fellows be assigned to the Office of Technology Assessment.

CHAPTER 3

A Perennial Source of Technical Expertise

The first two classes of science and engineering Fellows had done a great deal to demonstrate the practicality and value of the new program. The AAAS staff was already receiving many more expressions of interest from congressional offices than there were Fellows. None of the participating societies were having trouble recruiting highly capable Fellows from within their disciplinary ranks. To channel this momentum toward creating a perennial source of technical expertise for the legislative branch, the fellowship administrators believed their next priority must be to expand the coalition of professional societies and ensure a stable financial base.

American Psychological Association

AAAS Executive Officer William Bevan, Jr., who was trained as a psychologist, was personally committed to adding social and behavioral scientists to the congressional fellowship program. He targeted the American Psychological Association (APA) as a professional society that should join in the effort. Bevan laid out the fellowship program to APA President Albert Bandura and detailed the contributions of the first six Fellows. He explained AAAS's position that the program "should ultimately involve participants from practically all of the sciences, both natural and social and behavioral, and engineering," and invited APA to sponsor its own Fellows. In summarizing feedback received from users of the first class of Fellows, Bevan said that "some Congressmen expressed the thought that, while strongly supporting the program and desirous of possibly having the services of a trained professional scientist, their areas of need were 'too social-science oriented' to warrant the services of what they assumed were only natural scientist-fellows." He suggested that the need for social and behavioral scientists on congressional staffs was substantial, and that "the psychological community has much to offer in filling this need."[1]

The APA board of directors liked the idea of initiating an APA congressional fellowship program, but was reluctant to commit to the full yearly cost of sponsoring a Fellow, then set at $17,000. When AAAS secured an $8,500 grant from a small private foundation to sponsor a joint AAAS/APA psychology Fellow for 1974-75, the APA board agreed to provide the matching funds. So enabled, AAAS selected the psychologist Pamela Ebert to be the first AAAS/APA Fellow. She became the first science and engineering Fellow to work with the Senate Subcommittee on Children and Youth.[2]

Pleased with Ebert's contributions and the promise of a sustained fellowship program, APA assumed full funding for a psychology Fellow during the 1975-76 season. Lawrence Froman, who won the competition that year, landed an assignment with the Senate Committee on Labor and Human Resources. Like many of the physical scientist Fellows of that period, Froman found himself addressing legislative issues relating to energy policy. Among his various responsibilities was his staff assignment to Project Fuel, a proposed energy project that would be under either the Federal Energy Administration or the Community Services Administration, or both. Project Fuel intended to winterize the homes of the nation's elderly and poor. As a social scientist, Froman helped assess the needs associated with securing and maintaining community support for such a program.[3]

Scribner felt a good deal of pride about the fellowship program and reported to William Bevan that the growing number of societies ready to join the program "is witness not only to an idea whose time has come, but also to the importance of the central coordinating and leadership role of the AAAS." Scribner noted that 1974-75 "will be the second year that the program has proceeded as a more-or-less hand-to-mouth endeavor, although I believe it is not incorrect—though perhaps immodest—to say we have presented a fairly polished and well organized program exterior, all on rather small operating funds."[4]

In the program's third year, the Senate adopted a concurrent resolution that placed on record the Congress's appreciation to the professional societies that had already sponsored 37 science and engineering Fellows. The resolution underscored its praise by encouraging the societies "to continue and expand this vital public service activity."[5] Massachusetts Senator Edward Kennedy, in introducing the resolution on the floor of Congress, stressed that the 37 Fellows had come free of charge and that their donated salaries and benefits alone represented an amount "well over $1 million during the past three years." In commenting on his colleagues' enthusiasm for the program, Kennedy stated that "many more members have requested science and engineering fellows than could be accommodated by the limited number of individuals available."[6] Ohio Senator John Glenn added his praise: "It is generally well known on Capitol Hill that the science fellows have made a very positive contribution to the legislative process during their stay here in Washington," he said. "I agree with those sentiments as I know that we have drafted and passed much legislation that we might not have become knowledgeable about if they had not been present."[7]

Despite this enthusiastic reception within Congress, budgetary constraints made some of the participating professional societies reconsider their commitment to the fellowship program. In 1975, when William Bevan learned that the board of directors of the American Psychological Association was about to withdraw from the program, the former AAAS executive officer (who then held an endowed professorship in the department of psychology at Duke University) wrote to APA board Chairman Donald T. Campbell in an attempt to change its mind. Bevan understood the conflict within the psychological association: Should it spend its discretionary money to lobby Congress on behalf of psychology, or should it allocate those funds for its congressional fellowship program? Expressing his approval of the serious lobbying efforts then being undertaken by APA, Bevan nevertheless wanted Campbell to appreciate the broader political implications. "Lobbying is ultimately identified with parochial and self-serving interests," he advised. "The fellowship program is committed to the more fundamental notion that the long-range needs and goals of science can best be served by a colleagueship between scientist and lay decision maker, and by attention to the varied roles of science in advancing the public good than in putting forward the special interest of the guild. The welfare of science is best served by a better public understanding of science, and this understanding is best achieved by the education of the leadership in key segments of our society."[8] Bevan's argument—and those of like-minded advocates—proved persuasive, as the APA board of directors decided to retain the fellowship program.[9]

The Search for Foundation Support

William D. Carey replaced Bevan during the midst of the second fellowship year, and he, too, became a strong supporter of the program. As a former analyst with the U.S. Bureau of the Budget, Carey brought with him a keen sensitivity about the propriety of maintaining clear divisions between the public and private sectors. AAAS, of course, often bridged those worlds, and the congressional fellowship program was but one case in point. In soliciting a one-year grant from the Alfred P. Sloan Foundation in summer 1975, Carey assured Executive Vice President Robert Kreidler that "the program has ample safeguards against conflicts of interest." Moreover, he added that "modest financial assistance has been received from the business sector, but that avenue has been obstructed by lingering concerns as to possible criticism and misinterpretation."[10]

As with nearly all aspects of AAAS—and of most other nonprofit professional organizations, for that matter—fundraising was an ongoing concern. A successful track record made it easier to raise money for the fellowship program, but it did not alleviate the need altogether. The program's third anniversary seemed to arrive at a watershed moment. As the fellowship was on the cusp of establishing itself as a long-term, viable enterprise, it also faced an immediate financial crisis that threatened to slow its hard-won momentum. Sensing the importance of the situation, William Golden once again stepped forward with a personal donation, thereby allowing the AAAS congressional fellowship program to sidestep an otherwise troubling monetary snag.[11]

In November 1976, Carey turned to the Max C. Fleischmann Foundation for a two-year grant to fund a total of six congressional Fellows.[12] Widely recognized as one of science's most eloquent spokesmen, Carey had refined the rationale for the fellowship program based upon his own reflection and the results of the enterprise's first three years. The AAAS proposal to the Fleischmann Foundation stated: "Major issues before the Congress require greater in-office technical capability, especially with regard to the need for selective screening of pertinent scientific and technical information." The association, the proposal stressed,

> functions in a crucial central coordinating role and performs the necessary aggregation of the Fellows from various professional backgrounds with respect to the congressional openings. The single, focused approach that the AAAS provides gives to the Congress an image of one, single, tightly managed program, yet provides fluidity in the sponsorship and identification of the Fellows.

The congressional fellowship program was said to be an innovative aspect in the association's development of "its institutional capacity to provide critical information and assistance in the area of science and public policy." The proposal continued:

> Most of the pressing issues facing our nation for the foreseeable future will be related to major social problems such as energy, health, materials conservation, and improving our urban environment. Our national policy machinery, particularly within the Congress, is laboring as it tries to deal with the range of problems of choice. The pressure of very short response times in dealing with these issues and the difficulties which overloaded legislators have in separating fact from rhetoric in contentious areas highlight this inadequacy.
>
> Science and technology are crosscutting aspects of most of the intransigent problems on the legislative agenda. On its performance to date, the congressional policy

> machinery is plainly hard-pressed to cope with scientific and technical factors in decision making which bear directly on urgent national and transnational problems. This is not merely a temporary difficulty; it is a long-range one. Its solution calls for the orderly building of a professional capacity within as well as outside of the normal staff process.

The challenge facing Congress, according to AAAS, was in acquiring and utilizing the existing (and ever changing) scientific information. The expansion of the General Accounting Office and the Congressional Research Service, and the creation of the Office of Technology Assessment, were important steps in this direction, although, the AAAS argued, "the effective utilization of these resources by individual congressmen and committees requires an in-office capability.... Certainly, if the capabilities of science and technology are to play a greater role in shaping enlightened public policies, it is necessary that there be scientists and engineers who are familiar with the workings of government, who are prepared for leadership roles in policy-making positions in federal, state, and local government, and that there be a greater acceptance of the viability of such a career as an option for trained scientists and engineers." In promoting the science and engineering fellowship program, the AAAS proposal claimed that its principal benefit was contributions it made "at the margin where policy trade-offs and judgments must be made."[13]

Recruitment of Fellows

In their efforts to recruit outstanding applicants for the fellowship program, participating societies advertised widely in appropriate journals, magazines, and newsletters. The majority of applicants for the AAAS-funded fellowships said they learned about the program through notices in *Science* magazine. The second most cited source of information was word-of-mouth from former Fellows.[14] Individual scientists and engineers who applied to the program typically came from one of several motivated groups: people who wanted to change careers, leaving the world of research for the world of government service or an allied activity; people who had every intent of remaining researchers (presumably intending to return to their previous place of employment, or another like it, after the fellowship year) but who wanted the opportunity for meaningful public service and to learn more about the workings of government; and people whose career choices had not yet been made, because they had just graduated or were to graduate soon. Stephen Nelson, the fourth AAAS fellowship director, observed that the program tended to attract technically trained individuals who were willing to move outside the mainstream, traditional paths within their particular disciplines.[15]

AAAS's October 1974 fact sheet on the fellowship program spoke specifically to these motivations. In answering the rhetorical question Why is it needed? the association explained:

> Until recently, the scientific and technical community has remained aloof from much of the actual working mechanisms of government. Many scientists and engineers show an alarming lack of knowledge about the processes whereby governmental decisions are made. On the other hand, many scientists and engineers, often younger ones, today express genuine concern and interest in finding ways to utilize their knowledge for the betterment of society.
>
> Furthermore, it has frequently been noted that a gap exists which separates the political decision-making community from the scientific and technical communities. This separation stems from insufficient understanding, trust, and respect on both sides. Since science and technology are crucial elements in the solutions of many problems facing decision-makers and since this gap makes effective collaboration difficult, finding ways to reduce this separation is also a matter of prime concern to the AAAS.[16]

Stephen D. Ziman, a 1979-80 American Chemical Society Fellow assigned to the House Subcommittee on Science, Research, and Technology, had considered moving from his laboratory work as an industrial chemist to something involving the "industry/government interface" before he decided to apply for the fellowship. At the close of his fellowship year, Ziman's decision had been solidified; he reported his hope of returning to his previous employer (Chevron) to assist the firm in its government relations.[17]

Growing Pains

Working relations between the participating science and engineering societies and AAAS were generally quite good, but as with all such multiple, long-term interactions, differences occasionally arose among the organizations. Credit often loomed as a major concern among the member societies, who wanted—for obvious reasons—their sponsorship of congressional Fellows to be fully recognized. As a composite, overarching enterprise, the science and engineering fellowship program at times had the effect (sometimes real, sometimes perceived) of losing the individual societies within the whole. Such misperceptions tended to benefit AAAS, which, in its capacity as overall program administrator, was often credited for the entire operation by those unfamiliar with the program's internal structure.

Walter Ellis of the Federation of American Societies for Experimental Biology (FASEB), for example, voiced this concern at the December 1979 meeting of representatives of societies sponsoring Congressional Science and Engineering Fellows. Noting that one of the current FASEB Fellows was identifying himself as an AAAS Fellow rather than as a FASEB Fellow, Ellis pointed to AAAS's current advertisement for the fellowship program, which he believed fostered such misunderstanding by making the whole program look like the association's sole doing. Chiding AAAS for recently reducing the number of Fellows it was sponsoring from its own internal funds, Ellis asserted that "an ad like this looks like you are picking up the entire shooting match. You have converted a minimal investment into a $500,000 program."[18] Ellis's perceptions, while perhaps more passionately expressed than by any of his counterparts in the other participating societies, ensured that the AAAS staff redoubled its efforts to publicize the collaborative nature of the program and to share credit equitably.

As the fellowship program neared its 10th anniversary, other concerns began to crop up. Perhaps one of the most predictable tensions accompanied the expanding disciplinary diversity of the program. The program had grown from the original physical sciences and engineering members to include biological and social sciences members, and, in 1980, history and philosophy members. The stereotypical "two cultures" misunderstandings and differences, while not pronounced, were nevertheless unavoidable. When representatives of the participating organizations met in June 1980, several of the physical scientists and engineers expressed their "discomfort" with the growing diversity of the program, feeling that it was diluting the original goals and purposes of the enterprise. They worried, too, that the two-week orientation would have to be modified to meet the varying needs of the different disciplines. William G. Wells, Jr., who headed the AAAS fellowship office that year, defended the increased diversity, arguing that the orientation need not be greatly modified because "most of the kinds of things one needs to know about working on the Hill are independent of whether one is a psychologist or a physicist."[19]

J. Thomas Ratchford, who was then associate executive officer at AAAS, responded to American Physical Society (APS) Executive Secretary William W. Havens, Jr., who had been particularly vocal about this issue at the June meeting. "Perhaps this is the place to refer briefly to my own experience as a congressional Fellow," Ratchford wrote in a long, soothing letter. He said that as an American Political Science Association Congressional Fellow in 1968-69, he found himself to be the "token scientist" in that year's fellowship class. "I counted my contacts in that Fellowship year with the social scientists, reporters, lawyers, and others as a substantial asset," he counseled. "Sometimes we physicists tend to xenophobia, and exposure to lesser callings can serve a useful purpose. In any case, I would not have traded my 'multidisciplinary' orientation and seminar experience for the best 'physical science' one in the world."[20]

Ratchford's efforts, however well-meaning and sincere, did not quell the concerns of the APS. One year later, APS and AAAS representatives met again to discuss their disagreements, and again the physicists emphasized their displeasure with the fellowship's growing disciplinary diversity. As Richard Scribner, who had returned to the association after a two-year sabbatical at the State

Department, summarized their viewpoint, APS officials had "the perception that decisions made by AAAS are moving the program away from the more physical science and engineering focus it initially had, i.e., the perception that the program's image on the Hill is being diluted by the increasing number of behavioral scientists and four humanists in the group." Scribner claimed that the meeting had helped clear the air on this issue, but he worried that "it may remain a contentious matter."[21]

Differences, however, were not restricted to those between the physical scientists, on the one hand, and the humanists and behavioral scientists, on the other. During their internal deliberations about whether or not to sponsor their own congressional Fellows, officers of the American Geophysical Union (AGU) worried about the inclusion of engineering societies in the AAAS-administered program. "The only impurity in the other Associations now part of the program . . . would appear to me to be the inclusion of the ASME [American Society of Mechanical Engineers] and the 501C6 status of IEEE [Institute of Electrical and Electronics Engineers] as opposed to the 'public charity' status of the rest of the adhering organizations," wrote AGU's Joseph C. Cain in November 1976. "My own philosophy in this area is that it is very important even by implication to clearly separate 'science' from 'technology' or the 'applications' to which scientific results are put and that I would prefer to keep our organization on the 'science' side of the line. I would thus not normally recommend that our organization join engineering societies except on a temporary expediency."[22] AAAS was able to lay to rest the concerns of the geophysicists about the appropriateness of the joint venture by emphasizing the importance and value of integrating engineers fully with scientists. AGU joined the program in 1977 through the sponsorship of a single Fellow and has since remained a solid supporter of the program.[23]

A related concern that troubled some representatives from the participating societies during the 1980s was that the Fellows quickly lost their identity as scientists and engineers, being seen instead, as Stephen Nelson stated, as either "ex-scientists" or "proto-permanent staffers." The year-long series of seminars and dinners for the Fellows came to carry the additional burden of addressing that concern, at least subtly.[24]

Richard Krasnow, an MIT-trained physicist and one of the 1981-82 AAAS congressional Fellows, expressed his delight at having interacted with a variety of Fellows from different disciplines, yet he came away believing that the split between the two cultures might well lead to varying preferences in the fellowship placements. "One of the advantages of working in a subcommittee is the opportunity to focus on a few selected areas and get to know something in depth; this appeals to the academic," he said in his recommendations to future congressional Fellows. "However, working out of the member's office exposes one to the swirling political cross-currents, a heady experience that would be a pity to miss. This is particularly true for those Fellows who are more interested in the *process* rather than the content, e.g., historians, psychologists, etc. Hard-core technologists might enjoy a subcommittee environment better."[25]

CHAPTER 4

Individual Fellowship Programs

It is difficult to appreciate fully the internal dynamics of the collaborative Congressional Science and Engineering Fellowship Program without knowing something about the distinct, individual fellowship programs that comprised the overall mosaic. The social, political, and economic climate that had fostered and made possible American Society of Mechanical Engineers (ASME) and AAAS congressional fellowship programs (previously discussed) provided the same conducive atmosphere for other scientific and engineering organizations. The idea, it seemed, was in the air.

By 1993, 40 professional societies had participated in the enterprise by sponsoring one or more Fellows annually. Some of these societies linked arms with AAAS at the beginning and have remained steadfast partners to this day. Other societies started by establishing their own independent congressional fellowship programs, only later banding with the multi-organizational effort. Some societies joined the fellowship program in the late 1970s or 1980s and have remained active participants, while others who joined during this period later pulled out for one reason or another.

Both the Institute of Electrical and Electronics Engineers (IEEE) and the American Physical Society (APS), for example, held concurrent internal meetings in 1972 to debate the merits of establishing a congressional fellowship program. Both decided to go forward on a trial basis in the following year, in tandem with AAAS. As noted earlier, the American Society of Mechanical Engineers predated all other societies by placing its first Fellow in

January 1973. The American Chemical Society followed suit in 1974 and, like ASME, chose to operate its program independently for several years before officially linking with the collaborative, AAAS-administered program.

Sociologists and cultural anthropologists have long offered insights into the varying internal cultures, value systems, and behavior patterns of specialized organizations. Given the wide range of professional societies that have coalesced to form and maintain the Congressional Science and Engineering Fellowship Program, the differences of opinion, style, and action could at times be marked. To the outside world, however, whatever internal conflicts or disagreements that existed—or occasionally erupted—were essentially invisible, as the public face of the program was nearly always one of unquestioned unity.

To give a better sense of the multi-organizational character of the fellowship coalition, this chapter will briefly examine the congressional fellowship programs of six professional societies and the Office of Technology Assessment. In so doing, it will necessarily revisit some of the same events covered in previous chapters. I chose to discuss the following societies not because I believed them to be the most important or influential, but because I considered them representative of the range of disciplines and circumstances characteristic of the program's overall development.

American Physical Society

The AAAS-administered Congressional Science and Engineering Fellowship Program that was started in September 1973 enjoyed the close partnership of the American Physical Society (APS) and the Institute of Electrical and Electronics Engineers. Yet this was not necessarily the strategy the three had initially mapped out. Each organization had begun its internal deliberations by deciding whether it should create its own free-standing congressional fellowship program. Only later in spring 1973, when the leadership of the three societies began conferring amongst themselves, did they recognize that they would reap additional benefits by banding together and, perhaps, attracting other societies to join them in future years.[1]

Because Joel Primack was an avid congressional fellowship promoter and an activist member in both AAAS and APS, early discussions of forming fellowship programs within the two organizations followed similar paths. Primack, in fact, was one of the earliest advocates of merging the interested science and engineering societies in a commonly run operation. He lobbied the APS governing council, for example, claiming that "participation by the scientific societies will help to increase the professional prestige of the fellowship, a factor that will aid in recruitment of fellows, in their placement in Congress, and in their efforts to arrange leaves of absence from their scientific employment or to return to such positions at the conclusion of their fellowships."[2]

The APS's Forum on Physics and Society took the lead in promoting an APS congressional fellowship program. The forum created a special Committee on Congressional Fellows, chaired by Carleton College physicist Barry M. Casper.[3] In rationalizing the expenditure of APS funds for this new endeavor, Casper repeatedly stated that the congressional fellowship program would "serve notice that the American Physical Society seeks actively to promote public service activities among its membership by providing recognition and reward for such activities."[4] The APS governing council was duly impressed with the Casper Committee proposal. In January 1973 it approved the establishment of an APS Congressional Science Fellowship program, although funding was not immediately forthcoming.[5]

APS Executive Secretary William W. Havens, Jr., was initially skeptical about committing society resources toward the new fellowship. "I did not see how a few physics Ph.D.'s could have much influence on Congress," he wrote Casper. By April, however, he had been persuaded that the fellowship program could have an enormous positive impact on the physics community itself and "that by establishing a Congressional Science Fellowship the American Physical Society gives its blessing to this type of activity and encourages physicists to become engaged in the politics of science." Havens therefore encouraged Casper to "stress the fact that the APS is supporting the long-range goal of legitimizing for physicists activities other than traditional research in universities and industry.

In the long run, having some physicists with Congressional experience and possibly elected representatives in Congress will benefit physics as a whole and this is the job of the Society."[6]

Havens's endorsement was an important step toward realizing a successful program. Casper felt especially pleased about the improved prospects, as he took seriously the Forum on Physics and Society's goal of making "public policy work a legitimate professional activity of physicists." In his opinion, "the Congressional Science Fellowships will be the first major APS program of this sort."[7] The APS council agreed, and at the end of April it voted to finance up to two APS congressional science Fellows to join with the AAAS-administered program that was to be launched in September 1973.[8] Indeed, the success of the science and engineering fellowship program was indebted to the early and constant involvement of the physicists in this regard.[9]

As Harold Davis wrote in a 1973 *Physics Today* editorial, the American people had yet to elect a Ph.D. physicist as a member of Congress. Moreover, he said, out of a professional staff of nearly 2,000, only two Ph.D. physicists were serving the legislative branch in fall 1973: John Andelin (then administrative assistant to Washington Representative Mike McCormack) and J. Thomas Ratchford (then science consultant to the House Committee on Science and Astronautics). This placed Congress at a distinct disadvantage, Davis argued, because the executive branch employed many scientists and engineers.[10]

"The nearly complete lack of resident expertise on Congressional staffs is found not only in physics but in other sciences and areas of technology as well," Davis continued. "A modest-size business corporation faced with making million-dollar decisions typically has more specialists in science and technology on its staff than are available to Congressional Committees reaching decisions on billion-dollar questions. This historical deficiency is all the more glaring in these times when the impact of technology is apparent on all parts of our society. Today, any major legislative issue that comes before Congress is likely to involve an interaction with some area of science or technology. Clearly, Congress is forced to function under a distinct handicap if it has less than adequate advice in these areas."[11] He praised APS for initiating its congressional fellowship program.

"In the long run," Davis proclaimed, "we would hope to find many young physicists and other scientists aspiring to permanent careers with the Congressional staff or even as members of Congress. Congressional Fellowship programs that APS and other societies have wisely initiated represent a significant step toward encouraging this much-needed public service."[12]

The governing council of APS was pleased with the first year's fellowship class and approved funding two more Fellows for the second year, again working through the AAAS program.[13] When the selection committee became deadlocked on three equally outstanding applicants, however, the council agreed to fund yet a third Fellow for the 1974-75 fellowship year.[14]

Like other societies participating in the science and engineering fellowship program, the governing board of APS voted annually whether to continue allocating funds for the program. In so doing, it and the other societies were making an important statement and reaffirmation because they were committing the limited funds of their own members. To legitimize this commitment in a responsible manner, APS (again like other societies) also conducted periodic reviews of the program as a form of oversight.[15] These periodic reviews enabled the APS leadership to evaluate whether the congressional fellowship program was still fulfilling a need, whether it could be further improved, and whether the society should continue sponsoring it.[16] In assessing the impact of the physicists in November 1976, Scribner said that from his perspective

> the participation of the APS in this program has been one of the key anchor points in the whole Congressional Fellow effort. Without the support and cooperation of the American Physical Society back in the early stages of the program, it is problematic whether AAAS could have sustained its effort to date and been able to encourage six other professional societies to also join. The care exercised in the APS selection process, the quality of the Fellows selected, and the involvement of the Physical Society's leadership are standards all of the participating societies can look up to.[17]

The APS's 1987 report was thoroughly positive. The ad hoc review panel found that the society's members retained their confidence in the fellowship program and that congressional offices that had hosted APS Fellows were pleased and grateful. The panel recommended "that the Society continue to support the program as part of its public service activity, that the choice of Congressional affiliation be reserved to the Fellows, that mechanisms be developed whereby the Fellows can better contribute to the effectiveness of the Society's public service programs, and that another retrospective review be held in five years."[18]

The 1987 report recounted the physicists' original justification for supporting such a program in 1973—"public service by Society members and the return of information about the mechanisms of Congressional process to the members of the Society." The first goal—service to the Congress—had consistently been viewed by APS as having been achieved by the program, which had provided Congress with "useful technical analysis which might otherwise not be available." However, as early as the 1978 report, the second goal—transferring knowledge of Congress to the APS membership—was viewed as "unrealistic." The 1987 panel recommended articulating an additional, secondary goal for the program: to promote the society's public service contributions through the ongoing work of APS's *former* Fellows. As the panel noted: "The Fellows who remain with the Congress continue to provide technical support to the offices in which they serve. Those Fellows who enter government service, move to other public sector affiliations, or return to the industrial or academic sector often do so in posts where they call upon their Washington experience in the course of their work."[19]

Speaking to the integrity and effectiveness of the APS congressional fellowship program, the panel stated that "it will continue to be the responsibility of the selection committee to guard against candidates who would attempt to use the program to further personal goals." Moreover, the panel said that "to use the Fellows, by restricting their options for Congressional service or by requiring them to further a political agenda for the Society, would compromise the integrity of the program and destroy the effectiveness of the Fellows." The panel further recommended that "the program continue as a public service of the Society fully supported by its members," and that it not be funded through external grants, whose uncertainty had threatened the stability of congressional fellowship programs of other scientific and engineering societies, including AAAS's.[20]

The issue of the larger scientific community's perception of the fellowship program troubled APS as it had other participating societies, and indicated a perennial concern. According to the 1987 panel:

> Many of those who responded to the Panel's request for advice spoke to a continuing problem—the perception of the character of the program. All agreed that, if the physics community considers this program primarily a subsidized graceful exit from the physics "profession," it will not prosper. Inappropriate candidates will present themselves, and the program will not realize its secondary goals even if it meets its primary goal each year.
>
> The program provides opportunity for public service activity by physicists. They can, by using the analytical skills which they have learned and polished, and with reference to their own technical background or to that of colleagues, offer needed and valued help to the Congress which might otherwise not be available.
>
> It is true that the Fellowship year has sometimes been the occasion for a career change for a Fellow, that some of the Fellows have chosen a nontraditional milieu in which to practice physics, to contribute to the advancement and diffusion of the discipline. The contributions of these Fellows who "left" the laboratory are no less valuable than the contributions of those who "stay" in the laboratory.[21]

In the end, the panel asserted, the actual work and contributions of the Fellows speak for themselves. "The records of the Fellows, the work they accomplished during their year in Washington, the contributions they have made to the discipline of physics, to the community of scientists, and to society at large since their Fellowship year, engender respect and appreciation. The Society gets credit for expending its resources wisely in the public's interest."[22]

Four years later, APS's subsequent ad hoc fellowship review panel took much the same position, finding that "the Program continues to meet the Society's objective of providing a public service by making available individuals with scientific knowledge and skills to members of Congress. Through its Fellows, the Society assists in formulating policies having scientific content." The panel added that "the relationship of the Society to public servants in the Nation's capital is becoming of increasing significance. The past and present congressional Fellows can play an important role in helping the APS devise effective strategies in its outreach programs."[23]

Institute of Electrical and Electronics Engineers

The Institute of Electrical and Electronics Engineers (IEEE) had held internal discussions about creating a congressional fellowship program quite independently of AAAS or APS. In fact, it announced the establishment of its experimental program in the January 1973 issue of its official journal, the *IEEE Spectrum*, explaining that "the program is a direct response to the recent membership questionnaire, which expressed an interest in expanding the society's role into areas more responsive to the public interest to exert greater leadership in making technology the true servant of mankind." IEEE's Government Relations Committee took the administrative lead for the new program, which it openly admitted was "patterned after the successful experience of the American Political Science Association."[24]

Although inspired by political scientists, electrical engineers conceived of their fellowship program along lines very similar to those of their technical colleagues in AAAS and APS: engineering Fellows would serve for a full year on the staff of an individual congressional member or a committee or subcommittee; they would be entirely free to arrange their own placements and would have no official policy connection with IEEE. Electrical engineers maintained a couple of minor conceptual differences, however. For example, during the first year, IEEE sought to place its Fellow (or Fellows—

the option for sponsoring more than one was left open) with the Office of Technology Assessment (OTA), which was in the process of building its initial staff. Another variation was the expectation that the Fellows would have most or all of their stipends paid by their current employers, where they would presumably return to work after the close of their fellowship.[25] Neither of these contemplations materialized: Fellows were not placed with OTA and previous employers did not underwrite the entire cost of the program (although several supplemented the Fellows' stipends). Part of the leveling of approach no doubt arose with IEEE's banding with the AAAS-administered program that first year.

As with representatives of several other participating societies, IEEE's initial Fellows tended to work in the area of energy policy. For example, both Ronal W. Larson (1973-74) and Lloyd B. Craine (1974-75) concentrated on solar energy issues at the House Committee on Science and Technology. Anthony L. Rigas, the IEEE congressional Fellow for 1975-76, worked out of the personal office of Oregon Senator Bob Packwood, where he was appointed staff director of the Senate Republican Policy Committee Ad Hoc Task Force on Energy. Engineering Fellows seemed especially apt at assisting with energy and technology policy concerns, and they generally proved to be highly effective and desirable additions to congressional staffs.[26]

Despite contributions made by the early IEEE congressional engineering Fellows, by 1980 there emerged a number of critics who questioned the direct benefit of the program to the IEEE membership. P. Gene Smith, the 1979-80 IEEE Fellow, responded to the criticisms and to calls for measuring the success of the program, stating that he believed the effort was "very worthwhile and deserves the support of the membership." He claimed that "it is simply unrealistic to credit any legislative action solely to the efforts of such a small group [i.e., the IEEE Fellows]." A better gauge, he said, was to assess the numbers of engineers participating in congressional activities, either as staff members or witnesses. "My attitude is that nothing is more important to our country's future than the legislative process; we would be remiss to do less rather than more to try to improve this process, even if we cannot accurately measure our success in legislative terms or short-term value to the IEEE membership."[27]

American Chemical Society

To enhance broad participation by scientific and engineering societies, the AAAS staff sought to draw in some of the nation's largest scientific societies, which they hoped would set an example and solidify a needed core. The American Chemical Society (ACS) was one such targeted group. The Washington, D.C.-based ACS boasted of having the largest membership of any single-discipline scientific society. Moreover, it had a long-standing interest in assisting the government with public policy questions pertaining to chemistry and chemical engineering.[28]

Despite its size, ambitions, and active professional staff, ACS did not come to the idea of establishing a congressional fellowship program concurrently with ASME, IEEE, APS, and AAAS, but rather found itself reacting to the various programs being set in place in 1973. Following the April announcement of the new fellowship opportunity in *Science* magazine, Herman S. Bloch, chairman of the ACS board of directors, campaigned to get the chemical society to join the AAAS-orchestrated program by setting aside enough funds to finance one or two Fellows per year. "This program offers an opportunity for direct input of the viewpoint of the chemist to key congressional committees," he said, "and provides a means of doing so via a non-lobbying route." In preparation for the board's consideration later that spring, Bloch directed the ACS staff to gather information about the various science and engineering fellowship programs.[29]

Charles G. Overberger, chair of the ACS Committee on Chemistry and Public Affairs, immediately grasped the import of Bloch's recommendation and offered his full support, believing that any such endeavor would fall logically within the purview of his committee.[30] Within the society's headquarters, where the ACS Department of Chemistry and Public Affairs provided staff support to Overberger's committee, department director Stephen T. Quigley undertook reconnaissance on various congressional fellowship programs. Quigley reported that "there's been very little involvement of natural scientists until just recently." Following his description of the several "existing and planned programs," he noted that AAAS clearly "sees itself as the potential central administrator for any broad scientific and engineering Congressional Fellowship Program, similar to the position APSA has developed in the political science, law, and journalism areas." Quigley was not overly enthusiastic about the ACS's linking itself immediately with its sister organizations. "While the concept of all of these fellowship programs embodies the potential for broadening (on an individual basis) the perspective of both the scientific and the governmental communities regarding the value of scientific-governmental interactions," he said, "there is a real need to examine all the ramifications of such a program in terms of the relative effectiveness of the different mechanisms for introducing scientific and technical parameters into the government science and public policy formulation process."[31]

This caution was typical of the chemical society, which had historically been reluctant to join with others in cooperative ventures. The tendency to avoid giving up its prerogatives or sharing credit is perhaps characteristic of large organizations. It was especially a factor for ACS when it came to working with AAAS, as each sought to define its own role within the Washington, D.C., science policy community. For Quigley's part, his own Department of Chemistry and Public Affairs paralleled AAAS's Office of Science and Society (which Richard Scribner headed), so staking out territory was paramount in his thinking and that of his sponsoring committee members.[32] Commenting on his failed attempts to get ACS to initiate its own congressional fellowship program and to link it with the umbrella program being assembled by AAAS, Scribner told the association's treasurer, William Golden, that "the American Chemical Society still has a rather stand-offish posture, but I'm working on them."[33]

Wesley D. Bonds, Jr., of the chemistry department at Michigan State University, complained to the ACS leadership in 1974 about the "retiring manner" of the chemical society's public affairs office. "The ACS should be a leader in public affairs not a follower," he wrote.

> Perhaps we are too big and too diverse to make any significant stands in the public affairs area. But one thing is certain, the chemistry students at this school think that neither the ACS nor chemists as a group take the public

positions that other types of scientists are willing to adopt. ... Every week the stack of *Science* magazines being distributed into student mailboxes gets a little higher. That magazine contains little pure chemistry and almost no applied chemistry but I expect that student hours spent reading it will rival those spent reading C&EN [*Chemical & Engineering News*]. Clearly, these are a new group of people. They are not the "gee whiz" science buffs of the Sixties and Fifties. One of their interests seems to be public affairs and we don't seem to feed it.[34]

When the ACS board of directors met in August 1973 to act upon the congressional fellowship proposal, it voted to "approve in principle" the recommendation of the Committee on Chemistry and Public Affairs, rather than to support it outright. Cautious board members wanted to see a detailed budget before they committed society resources to the new initiative. The fellowship concept put forward by the committee and endorsed by the board differed in several ways from the science and engineering fellowship program administered by AAAS. Aside from its independent standing, the proposed ACS program would split the Fellows' time between the legislative and executive branches of government. According to the committee's proposal: "After a brief orientation period, each fellow would be assigned specific executive and legislative areas for research and liaison activities depending upon the individual's background, interests, and the needs of the department. Projects would be allocated so that the individual's time would be broken down equally among Senate, House of Representatives, and executive agency assignments."[35]

Although the ACS board approved the establishment of a Chemistry and Public Affairs Fellowship program[36] at its December 1973 meeting, the first Fellow—Renee G. Naves, a chemist from American University—did not start until 1975.[37] Instead of expecting Naves to negotiate her own assignment as did her colleagues in the parallel fellowship programs, ACS assumed responsibility for arranging her placements (the hope being to land three- to four-month assignments in the House, Senate, and an executive branch agency).[38] As science writer Constance Holden reported, ACS's Fellow was "kept on a shorter leash to ensure that his or her experience will be of benefit to the society, and is expected to participate in ACS affairs as well as government assignments."[39] Naves ended up splitting her fellowship year among appointments at the National Science Foundation, the personal office of Maryland Representative Gilbert Gude, and the House Committee on Science and Technology.[40]

When officials from the scientific and engineering societies that sponsored congressional Fellows convened in 1975 to assess their experiences, Stephen Quigley outlined ACS's independent Chemistry and Public Affairs Fellows program. The society's support was premised on the chemists' receiving due recognition, he said, as well as a "recognizable return from the program." He explained that ACS divided each fellowship among equal-lengthed assignments with the House, the Senate, and the executive branch as a preemptive strike against the possibility of the program's becoming a recruiting device for the Congress. Unlike some of the other societies, ACS preferred that all of its Fellows return to their previous jobs after their year on Capitol Hill, so that they might share their knowledge and insights with their colleagues and students.[41]

One year of the split-assignments approach was enough for the ACS leadership to see the advantages of full-term placements with the Congress. ACS's second Fellow, Bodo Diehn, spent his entire year with the legislative branch, although he held overlapping posts with the House and Senate, spending six months with the House Subcommittee on Consumer Protection and Finance (of the Committee on Interstate and Foreign Commerce) and 11 months with the Senate Committee on Aeronautical and Space Sciences.[42] Even though subsequent ACS Fellows followed work patterns similar to the multi-society Congressional Science and Engineering Fellowship program, the chemists turned down repeated invitations to link forces with their sister organizations, opting instead to go it alone. Nevertheless, the stated objectives of the ACS fellowship program differed little from those of its counterparts: "to provide an opportunity for scientists to spend a year gaining firsthand knowledge of how the federal government works, to make available to government an increased amount of scientific expertise, and to give scientific and government personnel better acquaintance with what each can contribute to the development of public policy."[43]

The ACS Department of Chemistry and Public Affairs stood firm in the independent path of its fellowship program through spring 1978, when Quigley left the society for a job in the Pentagon and a commission as a Navy admiral.[44] Later that year, the chemists formally joined the collaborative effort. In 1979, they expanded their program from one Fellow per year to two. Thomas H. Althuis became the first ACS Congressional Fellow to participate fully in the AAAS-administered program. As he reported to the ACS Committee on Chemistry and Public Affairs, the affiliation with the broader program had distinct advantages. "During the interviews I found that most offices on the Hill were unaware that the ACS sponsored congressional science fellows," he said.

> Most thought I was the first ACS fellow. Placing more emphasis on the term ACS Congressional Fellow has given the program more direct meaning to the Hill, rather than the term Chemistry and Public Affairs Fellow, which to those who know no more, does not convey a congressional fellowship. By association with AAAS the ACS fellowship program has received extra publicity and contacts. AAAS association may also improve the program in the view of ACS members.
>
> The move toward the AAAS has been very worthwhile not only because of the orientation program and the added recognition it gives the ACS Congressional Fellow on the Hill but also the contact with other congressional Fellows.[45]

Like other scientific and engineering societies that sponsored congressional Fellows, ACS became concerned about effectively utilizing the substantial resource its former Fellows represented. The chemists had sponsored 15 congressional Fellows by 1983, yet they had failed to establish any formal program "in which former fellows can contribute, based on experiences from Capitol Hill, to the Society after the expiration of the fellowship." Former Fellows proposed the "development of a Fellows Network to provide a bank of scientific expertise and an entree to congressional and agency contacts." The Congressional alumni stressed that they could assist ACS "in getting chemistry perceived on the Hill as the 'central science.'"[46]

Despite the success of the science and engineering fellowship program in general, and the ACS-sponsored Fellows in particular, the ongoing stability of the chemical society's fellowship program was not something that could be taken for granted. Instead of rousing high praise and resolve on the part of the ACS leadership on the ten-year anniversary of the program in 1984-85, some board members began questioning the wisdom of continuing to support this endeavor.[47]

Chemists, perhaps more than scientists in other disciplines, felt besieged in the 1970s and 1980s by critics who often equated various environmental problems with the contributions of chemists and the chemical industry. This led to a certain degree of defensiveness. The congressional Fellows program offered a tangible way to combat this perceived situation. As ACS staff members Annette Rosenblum and Mary Wolfe argued when highlighting the value of placing chemistry Fellows on Capitol Hill: "When the news media headline a story about a chemical spill, a local government that has detected contaminated groundwater, or a hostile takeover of a petroleum company, pressure is brought to bear on lawmakers in Washington to find a solution."[48]

ACS staff worked to portray their congressional fellowship program as a proactive service to the society's members and the chemistry community in general. To gain visibility, they periodically ran stories in the society's weekly news magazine, *Chemical & Engineering News*, about a particular Fellow or the program as a whole.[49] By 1986, ACS had sponsored 16 congressional Fellows. When polled, chemistry Fellows reported that "the fellowship year was one of the most exciting, professionally rewarding, and educational years of their lives." Two of these former Fellows continued to work for Congress, one went to work for the executive branch, two joined chemical associations, six were employed in industry, and four returned to academic appointments. According to ACS, "most of them are involved with some aspect of government relations or science and technology policy."[50]

Because the congressional Fellows program depended on annual reauthorization and funding by the ACS's board of directors, internal support was crucial. Each year the program would surface before the board (whose membership rotated on a regular basis), who then voted whether to extend the program and allocate funds. For a variety of reasons, the chemists' commitment to the fellowship program wavered over time. From 1974 to 1979, ACS sponsored one Fellow per year; from 1979 to 1987, it sponsored two Fellows per year; from 1987 to 1990, it dropped back to one; and in 1990 it suspended the program altogether, only to revive it two years later. This naturally concerned the AAAS leadership. In 1985, for example, AAAS Executive Officer William Carey wrote his ACS counterpart, John K Crum, about a rumor that the chemists were considering cutting the number of congressional Fellows from two to one per year. "I hope you'll do your best to avert this," Carey wrote. "The ACS presence in the program is not only consistently first-rate, but it sends a strong signal of the value of the Fellows initiative to other participating scientific societies. We have something very important going on here—one of the few solid, productive, and visible linkages between the scientific community and the Congressional process. Both of us know that we are going to need every bit of help that we can get, over the next several years, to assure reasonable stability in the government *cum* science relationship in the face of oncoming pressures. I hope very much that ACS and AAAS can continue to stand together in keeping the Fellows program intact."[51]

Carey's effort bore fruit. Crum had distributed Carey's missive to the ACS board of directors, who subsequently voted to reinstate the full amount to the fellowship program, keeping the annual number of Fellows at two. Crum thanked Carey for his actions and told him to "count on us, if support for the AAAS program is ever needed."[52]

The averted halving of the chemists' fellowship program paled in comparison to the crisis that arose in 1989, when the ACS board of directors placed the entire program on the chopping block. Stephen Nelson, who was then running the overall Congressional Science and Engineering Fellowship Program, urged AAAS's new executive officer, Richard Nicholson, to do whatever he could to stem this threat. Nelson's recommendations suggest the activist stance taken by the AAAS staff on behalf of the program. "As the world's largest single discipline scientific society (137,000 members), ACS's continued involvement in the congressional Fellows program is important to AAAS," Nelson told Nicholson. "If they do not value the program sufficiently to continue to find $30,000 to $40,000 for it in an overall association budget of approximately $150 million, this could send a disturbing signal to several of the smaller societies who have to fight to come up with funds for their own Congressional Fellows."[53]

Concern over budgetary shortfalls had prompted the ACS board to eliminate several programs. As Nelson wrote Nicholson, the irony of axing the congressional fellowships was that "this action severs the one program that gives ACS some credibility on the Hill." Nelson thought the ACS fellowship program was surely doomed without quick and direct AAAS intervention. He recommended that Nicholson write directly to ACS Executive Director John Crum, encouraging continuation of the program in much the same manner that Carey had written only four years earlier. (Nelson suggested that Nicholson's training as a chemist and his longstanding ACS membership might carry added weight.) Nelson himself would try to rally the former ACS congressional Fellows to lobby ACS officers and board members on behalf of the program. Finally, passing along suggestions given to him by the current class of Fellows, he urged AAAS to solicit the support of Eugene Garfield, president of the Institute for Scientific Information and publisher of *The Scientist*, who was known to be sympathetic to the science and engineering fellowship program and who was himself a chemist.[54]

Support within ACS for the fellowship program remained weak, however, and by the end of October Crum sent Nicholson a formal letter outlining the situation. Despite the chemists' appreciation of the program and the manner in which AAAS had managed it, the ACS executive director stated that "because of current budgetary constraints, it would appear that the Society will be unable to continue our Congressional Fellowship program after the 1989-90 Fellow's term is completed." He left room for a change of heart, however, assuring his AAAS counterpart that if the society's board later reversed its decision, "the ACS hopes to be able to resume its role as an active participant within your program."[55]

Nicholson was not comforted. It was ironic, he told Crum, that at the same time the ACS board of directors decided to discontinue its congressional fellowship program, the AAAS board of directors asked to have the stipends of its congressional Fellows raised. "It is kind of amazing to me that our two organizations could come to such different conclusions," he said. Nicholson sympathized with the budget constraints facing the chemical society, yet he insisted that dissolving the fellowship program was a mistake. "My concern is more than just the loss of the ACS Fellows, of course, because I fear that with ACS's leadership position among the scientific societies, other participants may be influenced by your decision." It was his opinion, he told Crum, that *"in the long run,* it is people that make the difference and thus the various Fellows programs may be among the most significant activities that the scientific societies support, provided they are willing to take the long view. Certainly a review of the career path of past Fellows will show that many have gone on to key policy positions."[56]

Former ACS Fellows joined the lobbying effort to save the program, largely by soliciting letters of support from members of Congress. Tennessee Senator Albert Gore, Jr., who was then hosting ACS Fellow Kathleen McGinty, was one of the first to respond. Writing to ACS President Clayton F. Callis, Gore summarized the contributions of three ACS Fellows who had worked for him. Asking the chemical society to reconsider its decision, he asserted that "ACS Fellows are an invaluable resource to Congressional staffs studying science and technology issues—issues which I am sure you agree are crucial to the future well-being of our nation and our planet." He warned that "discontinuation of the Program—and our concomitant loss of the insights and perspectives of your talented chemists—would be a very serious detriment to our ongoing work on science and technology issues."[57]

Callis's response to the senator revealed the trade-offs that were being considered within the chemical society. The ACS president expressed his sympathy with the fellowship program, but explained that "the Society feels that based upon current financial constraints within the ACS and upon the need to divert our funds to tackle some of the long-term problems that we are trying to address, that some of our very good programs must be put on the 'back burner.'" Among those competing programs, Callis noted that "the American Chemical Society is making a wholehearted commitment to increase the scientific literacy of the general public through the U.S. educational system and to influence the public understanding of the chemical sciences through such mechanisms as a joint ACS/Smithsonian Exhibit." He told Gore, however, that ACS would revisit the fellowship program and that it might possibly reinstate it.[58]

The controversy raised by the board's termination of the congressional fellowship program prompted ACS's Committee on Chemistry and Public Affairs to conduct an internal audit of the program. Christopher T. Hill, then a senior staff member at the National Academy of Engineering, headed the investigation. Hill's report identified a number of perceived problems, but argued that the program's contributions far outweighed its costs. Therefore, he recommended that the board of directors reinstate the fellowship in the next year's budget.[59]

The internal audit and concerted campaign to revive the chemists' fellowship program proved effective. In 1991, the ACS board of directors reversed its earlier decision and voted to reinstate the program for the 1992-93 term. The board agreed to fund one fellowship in 1992 and promised to consider adding a second slot the following year.[60]

Patricia A. Cunniff, chair of the Subcommittee on Public Policy for the ACS Committee on Chemistry and Public Affairs, was instrumental in orchestrating the internal efforts to restore the fellowship program. In presenting an overview of the program in August 1991, she stressed that many other scientific societies—all of them with lower memberships—had been finding ways to fund congressional Fellows. As the world's largest single-discipline scientific organization, she said, ACS should be able to support at least a modest program.[61]

Office of Technology Assessment

The Office of Technology Assessment (OTA), which was established by law in 1972 and began functioning two years later, seemed a natural venue for the new science and engineering Fellows.[62] Advocates for OTA and the fellowship program shared the premise that Congress must deal with a broad spectrum of public policy questions that encompass significant scientific and technical elements, and that the legislators would be well served by having scientists and engineers examine and advise upon these issues. A few of the first-year Fellows had hoped to secure assignments with OTA, but no options were open to them in the early fall of 1973 because OTA was not funded until November. It did not really get its projects under way until the following year.[63] A perception held by Fellows was that their training, experience, and problem-solving approaches would be more fully appreciated and utilized in an organization specifically chartered to address science and technology-based policy concerns through the production of lengthy, analytical assessments. Others, such as John Andelin, believed it a misappropriation of scarce resources to place science and engineering Fellows with OTA, given that the office enjoyed a healthy budget to hire just such people. The real need, he and others argued, remained in the congressional members' and committee offices, where precious few technically trained people had ever worked as staff members.[64]

Although there was little initial discussion of placing science and engineering Fellows with OTA, the awareness of the commonalities of the two programs was always keen. Moreover, OTA's first director, former representative and House Science Committee stalwart Emilio Q. Daddario, was considered an important inside supporter (if not promoter) of the fellowship program, and the AAAS staff was not bashful about asking for his help.[65] And "Mim" Daddario proved more than happy to lend a hand. "I know of no other program which better informs young people about the workings of Congress specifically and government generally," he wrote in support of the fellowship program. "Beyond that, its purpose is to mold future leaders who will impact our society, and this the program is most certainly doing. This program has my wholehearted support, and I am ready to be of any assistance that I can to certify its necessity."[66]

Daddario followed up by raising the prospect of initiating a fellowship program before OTA's governing body, the Technology

Assessment Board, which eagerly endorsed the idea. With the board's green light, Daddario explored funding possibilities with McGeorge Bundy at the Ford Foundation, then passed on the encouraging information to William Bevan.[67] AAAS lost no time in submitting a proposal. In April 1974, the Ford Foundation approved the association's $102,000 grant request to fund three Fellows per year, for two years, to work specifically for OTA. In announcing the grant, the Ford Foundation stated that the funds were meant "to help build a corps of young scientists who will pursue careers along the interface of science and public policy."[68] *Science* magazine, however, reported Ford officials as stating that the foundation "is not particularly involved in science and that its chief interest in this case is helping a new government agency get off to a propitious start."[69] The AAAS/OTA Fellows would be grouped with the other science and engineering Fellows and receive the same orientation, the only difference being that placements for AAAS/OTA Fellows were restricted to OTA. As with other AAAS congressional Fellows, AAAS advertised the program and handled the selection, orientation, and administration of the Fellows. For its part, the Ford Foundation made clear that its grant was nonrenewable.[70]

The first Fellows assigned to OTA found themselves in an agency struggling to find its voice and niche within the congressional structure. It was an exploratory endeavor, as OTA's senior management and congressional overseers worked together to establish procedural mechanisms and to chart the office's overall course. Science and engineering Fellows placed within individual members' offices or within committees and subcommittees entered established organizations that, while often reactive and appearing to be loosely structured, had established routines. Early OTA Fellows, however, faced an uncertain situation.

Jerome Paul Harper was among the first OTA Fellows. In his final report, the young engineer wrote: "At OTA there was an existing scientific manpower pool before the fellows arrived. This situation is very different from other offices in the Congress, where a scientific capability is lacking. As a consequence, I felt somewhat less instrumental and perceived fewer opportunities at OTA than did fellows who had been placed in different offices."[71] Harper's colleague in 1974-75, Gary L. Thomas, worked on an assessment of strategic materials. Thomas, who was also an engineer, said: "The problems with the year stem from the same origin: I was there for only one year. Since I would not be able to finish the assessment, I was never given as much authority or responsibility as I wanted and needed to do the assessment properly. This led to a certain amount of frustration."[72]

The six Ford Foundation-funded Fellows received a warm welcome within OTA, yet AAAS was unable to secure continued funding for this particular fellowship, nor was it willing to allocate its own internal funds for an OTA-only fellowship. OTA, however, found the Fellows so valuable that it committed part of its own budget to start an independent fellowship program in 1978. As with the other affiliated fellowship programs, OTA ran its own selection process and paid AAAS an administrative fee to provide the orientation and follow-up services. During the first three years, OTA compensated the Fellows as contractors, an arrangement that left them responsible for obtaining their own health and life insurance, paying self-employment taxes, and the like. Thereafter, OTA retained its Fellows as though they were regular, temporary staff members, thereby granting them all the accompanying benefits of government employment.[73]

Despite the fact that OTA Fellows were grouped together with science and technology Fellows, fully participating in the orientation sessions and year-long series of dinner seminars and social events, their experiences were in many ways quite different from those of their colleagues. John Andelin, who served as a senior OTA administrator for over 10 years, claimed that OTA Fellows really held little in common with other Fellows. On one level, the OTA program operated more as a prestigious recruitment tool than it did as a straightforward fellowship program. OTA screened all of the applicants and decided which candidates to bring on board to work on particular projects. (One of the selection criteria was that each Fellow be linked to a project from the start. Fellowship candidates deemed superior on all other grounds, but who did not match the specific needs of OTA at that moment, would not be offered an appointment.) In this sense, OTA Fellows were "hired" for a specific task. They did not enjoy the latitude of the other science and engineering Fellows who were selected independently of any fit with a particular office or project and who were later completely free to negotiate their own placements.[74]

The practice of asking Fellows to spend the entire year working on a single project began in 1983. For the five previous years, OTA Fellows had divided their year among several projects, an arrangement that proved unsatisfactory for OTA officials and Fellows alike, given the substantive and in-depth nature of most OTA assessments.[75] Noting the difference between the other science and engineering Fellows and those at OTA, Andelin stressed that the single-project commitment meant that OTA Fellows typically learned a great deal about a narrow slice of a public policy issue, but gained far less insight into the legislative process, the Congress as a whole, or broad issues of science and technology policy.[76]

What really set the OTA fellowships off from those sponsored by the independent science and engineering societies, however, was the conscious use of the fellowship program for staff recruitment. At the end of the fellowship year, OTA attempted to retain those Fellows who had worked out well. If the relationship was not mutually satisfactory, no offer was made and the Fellows left. As OTA's personnel director William Norris observed, the fellowship program "has provided OTA with some really exceptional talent; many of the Fellows have stayed on and have assumed leadership roles."[77]

In addition to providing outstanding staff, the OTA fellowship program, which was renamed the Morris K. Udall OTA Congressional Fellowship Program in 1991 as a way to honor the long-time Technology Assessment Board member upon his retirement from Congress, also helped publicize OTA to the broader scientific and technical world. Norris said that this was especially important during the late 1970s and early 1980s when fewer people were aware of OTA's existence or the nature of its work. The national mailings announcing the annual fellowship competition were viewed by OTA officials as an effective means of advertising the organization to an important, targeted audience. By the 1990s, OTA had expanded its two-page flier into a four-page brochure, with the middle two pages solely a description of the organization, intended to enhance public understanding and awareness of the office's mission and approach.[78]

Society for Research in Child Development

As the Congressional Science and Engineering Fellows Program became firmly established in the mid-1970s, AAAS staff routinely looked to expand the number of Fellows and sponsoring societies. Child health policy was one area that provided an obvious match between the need for technical expertise within Congress and the availability of professionals within the research and practitioner communities.

Beginning in 1976, friends of and participants within the Fellows program began to explore ways to establish a special child health policy Fellows cohort. In January 1977, William Bevan approached the William T. Grant Foundation of New York with the idea of funding three child health policy congressional Fellows per year. "I would lean toward AAAS as the management group," Bevan told Grant Foundation President Philip Sapir. "The Association is strongly committed to the program, has extensive ties on the Hill, and does a good job of overseeing the program. In addition, it would insure the integration of your Fellows with others in the program—and the esprit that comes with being included and involved with the larger group of Fellows."[79]

Sapir was taken by the idea, and he began negotiating with AAAS about how best to set up such a program. As he told Richard Scribner, he believed it best to have the child policy Fellows administered by AAAS. On the other hand, he was hesitant to place the programmatic responsibilities in the hands of "any one discipline-oriented professional organization since there really is none that covers the breadth of disciplines that would and should be represented." To assist Congress with its activities in the area of national policy for children and youth, Sapir was committed to bringing in Fellows drawn from a number of disciplines, such as psychology, sociology, anthropology, economics, child psychiatry, pediatrics, family medicine, and social work.[80]

Hoping to strengthen the proposed child development Fellows program by securing a diversity of funding sources, AAAS looked to other organizations to supplement whatever resources might be forthcoming from the Grant Foundation. In July 1977, the AAAS succeeded in winning a three-year grant from the Foundation for Child Development, which agreed to fund one congressional Fellow in child development per year.[81]

Thus, the Congressional Science Fellows in Child Development was started in 1978 with four Fellows, all of them selected through a search process established and administered by AAAS. This particular fellowship shifted its operational responsibility to the Society for Research in Child Development (SRCD), which assumed the logistical and financial tasks of advertising and selecting the child development Fellows beginning with the second year, while AAAS continued to administer the Fellows' year in Washington.[82]

SRCD proved a natural home for the fellowship because of its interdisciplinary base. The society maintained "a commitment to communication across the scientific and professional fields whose interests center on child development," said Alberta Siegel, a professor of psychology at the Stanford University Medical Center and an SRCD official. "Our members include developmental psychologists, anthropologists, child psychiatrists, sociologists, pediatricians, and early childhood educators."[83]

In 1980, as the first three-year block grants were about to expire and SRCD began preparing to reapply for financial support, officials began considering how the child development fellowship might be modified. Several SRCD members wanted increased influence over where the Fellows worked within Congress. This more active role in the placement process—developing lists of congressional members considered most appropriate for child development Fellows to assist—troubled the AAAS staff, who warned that such involvement might lead to the impression that SRCD was acting as a lobbying group.[84]

Nevertheless, as SRCD's Karen Fischer explained, the society was committed to developing "methods of ensuring that Child Development Fellows actually achieve placements appropriate for advancing the objectives of the Fellowship program and specifically serve in offices that are pivotal to the development of legislation related to children, youth and families." SRCD conceded to allow its Fellows to work through the AAAS placement procedures, but the society insisted on giving its Fellows its own list of suggested offices and, beginning with the 1981-82 fellowship year, reserving the right to veto placements of its Fellows that SRCD considered inappropriate.[85]

In 1987, the Foundation for Child Development and the William T. Grant Foundation informed SRCD that, despite their positive view of the Congressional Science Fellowship in Child Development, they would not provide additional funding. This left the society with the tough decision of whether it considered the program worthy of continuation through its own internal revenues. As Deborah Phillips of the University of Virginia stated in a report to SRCD, "a central issue concerns whether the program (even if successful) has completed its effective lifespan. Some goals, once achieved, no longer require continued support; other goals are established in the context of constantly changing conditions, thus require ongoing support."[86] To the disappointment of the collaborating science and engineering societies, the SRCD leadership chose to fold its fellowship program.

The Humanist Members

The Congressional Science and Engineering Fellowship Program gained two of its most unlikely participating organizations in 1980: the American Philosophical Association (APA) and the American Historical Association (AHA). The late 1970s found newly trained humanists facing a serious job crisis. One response to this situation was the development of the "public history" movement, which looked beyond the halls of academe for meaningful employment opportunities.[87] The congressional fellowship idea appealed to this search for alternative careers among many of the younger APA and AHA members.

Although there was no "public philosophy" movement to match that of the historians, it was nevertheless the philosophers who took the lead in promoting the joint congressional fellowship idea. Prior to submitting their grant proposal to the Andrew W. Mellon Foundation, the philosophers and historians met with AAAS staff to discuss availing themselves of the orientation, placement, and administrative services of the, by then, highly regarded Congressional Science and Engineering Fellowship Program. Having worked hard to expand its own fellowship coalition, the AAAS staff welcomed the opportunity to add four more participants per year, even if they were not natural scientists or engineers. So, in August 1979, the two humanities associations submitted their request to Mellon for a three-year block grant, assuring the foundation that they would be able to participate in the AAAS-run program.[88]

The humanists, of course, had also considered the American Political Science Association's Congressional Fellowship Program, but concluded that the logistical practices of the AAAS program—with its full-year assignments—were superior. Such deliberations, however, were not voiced to the Mellon Foundation. "In recent years there has been a renewed recognition of the complexity of governmental decision making and of the human and moral components that coexist with more 'technical' dimensions of public policy issues," the associations argued in their joint proposal. "Scholars in such humanistic disciplines as history and philosophy have begun to turn to consideration of these issues."[89]

The Mellon Foundation officials were convinced, and in October 1979 they awarded APA and AHA their full grant requests (enough to fund two Fellows per year per association), so that their fellowship programs might begin in September of the following year.[90] The historians and philosophers who eventually served as congressional Fellows participated fully in the orientation program and ongoing events along with the scientists and engineers. No special training or programs were developed for them by AAAS, although APA and AHA were encouraged to follow the practice of the social scientists and have "break-out" sessions on issues of particular interest to their Fellows.[91]

The humanists shared a fundamental belief with other participating organizations in the congressional fellowship program: their programs served multiple objectives, bringing benefits to

Congress, the Fellows, and their disciplines alike. Melvin Kranzberg, a member of the AHA congressional fellowship selection committee, articulated this objective to his colleagues. "Not only do we want to insert historical parameters into Congressmen's thinking on the issues," he argued, "but we also want this experience to contribute to the candidate's intellectual and scholarly development, in terms of his/her future research and/or teaching."[92] Beyond the admittedly narrow aspect of developing alternative career options for historians, Kranzberg fully believed that historians had something important to offer Congress and that it was therefore incumbent upon them to pursue such service. "Congressional staffs are constantly preparing background materials dealing with the histories of various problems which present themselves to the Congress," Kranzberg told the AHA's executive director. "What I am trying to say is that, while the historians need this kind of employment, this kind of employment also needs historians!"[93]

In 1981, E. Lee Marmon, who oversaw AHA's congressional Fellows program, said: "Even though the AHA was able to sponsor only two fellows this year, we're hoping that there will be a trickle-down effect, that members of Congress will talk to other members about the program and begin to look more seriously at employing humanists where only political scientists in the past were expected to perform well."[94]

Kranzberg found numerous occasions to push for the continuation and expansion of the AHA fellowship program. Countering his colleagues who expressed concern that former Fellows might turn away from traditional academic employment, he argued that "if we 'lose' some of them to government pursuits rather than academia, this too benefits the historical profession by showing how history can be of immediate service to the nation." Urging the historical leadership to keep their eyes upon the larger issues, Kranzberg observed that "scientists are stepping out of their 'ivory laboratories,' and it is time that we historians came out of our 'ivory towers.' The AHA Congressional Fellowship Program is a major step in that direction."[95]

Because of the dearth of scientists and engineers working for Congress, it did not surprise many of the early science and engineering Fellows when their placement interviews produced quizzical looks on the faces of staff directors who had not previously considered how they might use technically trained personnel. The humanist Fellows, on the other hand, came with different expectations. Surely, they thought, members of Congress and their staffs would be comfortable with—if not conversant in—the disciplines of history and philosophy. But such was not always the case. The 1981-82 AHA Congressional Fellow, David W. Reinhard, spent a fruitful and mutually satisfying year on the personal staff of Pennsylvania Representative Joseph M. McDade. Yet, when he thought back to the placement process, he remained bewildered by the overall reception he received. "For reasons that still escape me after more than a year," he confessed, "a law degree remains the ticket into many job interviews on the Hill. A doctorate, on the other hand, elicits only awe and befuddlement. In short, a Ph.D. in history can be an obstacle to overcome."[96]

Stanislaus J. Dundon, an assistant professor of philosophy at California Polytechnic State University who taught courses on the history and philosophy of science, was one of the first APA congressional Fellows. Dundon joined the staff of California Representative George E. Brown, where he focused his attention on policy questions revolving around agriculture and hunger.[97] When asked about Dundon's contributions midway through his fellowship, Brown's administrative assistant, Timothy Lynch, said that Brown had been looking for someone with fresh views. "Dundon's experience and perspective as a philosopher is different and now, after nine months of working closely with him, we've come to rely on it. The kinds of interest groups he gravitates toward, the books he reads and the journals he cites, the recommendations he has on priorities, and the questions he raises during hearings form a uniquely humanistic perspective. His goals are fundamentally the same as ours. They're just articulated differently. Brown finds that very refreshing."[98]

As the originators of the joint humanities fellowship, the philosophers took the lead midway through the first three-year grant to look for additional sources of funding.[99] AHA's new executive director, Samuel R. Gammon, appreciated the program, but it was not at the top of his priorities list, meaning that he was not about to push his association to commit its own resources toward the effort. "We too have been eyeing the approaching end of the Mellon grant and are resolved to seek fresh funding," he wrote his APA counterpart. "Unfortunately," he added, "without new funds we will have to halt the program, since historians are in tight straits financially these days."[100]

In their successful bid to secure a three-year renewal grant from the Mellon Foundation, APA and AHA offered their considered view of the program, which was then entering its third year. "The expansion of the number of truly knowledgeable university teachers is an important tool to offset the growth of disillusionment among students with the federal government," they asserted. "That disenchantment stems in large part from the apparent discrepancy between textbook models and observed behavior patterns, not adequately explainable by inexperienced teachers." Former congressional Fellows, they claimed, would help remedy this situation. Like many of the natural scientists and engineers with whom they had joined, the philosophers and historians considered themselves unappreciated outsiders when it came to government policy making. As they told the Mellon Foundation, there is a problem with "the fact that humanists, unlike social scientists and lawyers, have for too long been seen by many to have little of value to contribute to issues of public policy." While grounded in examples of practical benefits of an extended fellowship program, the APA/AHA grant proposal said very little about the importance of service or of the social obligations of humanists; nor did it express a general tone of idealism so imbued in the original AAAS, APS, and IEEE discussions of 1973.[101]

When the Mellon Foundation renewed their grant for another three years, APA and AHA turned to the Rockefeller Foundation to request matching funds so that each association might add a third congressional Fellow. The point, they argued, was "to create better bridges between our two humanities' disciplines and the process of government."[102] Rockefeller obliged, but with a strictly unrenewable grant.

When the Mellon and Rockefeller monies ran out at the close of the 1985-86 fellowship year, neither APA nor AHA had found other external funding sources. They both let the project come to an end. Gammon had suggested as much to the Rockefeller Foundation in August 1985 when he wrote: "Although we will probably have to give the fellows program a rest after the coming year with the exhaustion of our current funding, we hope to revive it in the future."[103]

One problem that had plagued AHA was the declining number of applicants. When the program started, 52 historians applied to become congressional Fellows. That number dropped to 19 the following year, then rose to 21 in 1982, only to fall in the next cycle to 16 and to half that number in 1984.[104] Senate historian Donald A. Ritchie, who sat on the selection committee, expressed his concern to Gammon. "Considering how successful the program has been, and how much credit it reflects on the AHA, I cannot understand why it has not been advertised more extensively," Ritchie prodded. "At a time when jobs are still in short supply, we need to let people know these three positions are available."[105] Gammon agreed to beef up the association's advertising, but blamed much of the decline on the ingrained prejudices of their fellow historians. "I fear that what we are up against is partly the herd-bound instincts of many of our academicians," he said.[106]

The fellowship selection committee, however, was not satisfied with that explanation, preferring to analyze the multitude of variables they thought were warding off larger numbers of applicants. Such variables included the shrinking pool of junior faculty and matriculating Ph.D.s, the probability that the fellowship was still not widely known, and "the possibility that fewer potential applicants believe that they can now live in the Washington area on the $18,000 stipend."[107]

The humanists ultimately allowed their fellowship programs to end for three basic reasons—declining applications, end of the grant monies, and shifting priorities of the associations.[108]

CHAPTER 5

Assessing the Impacts on Congress, Fellows, and Sponsors

Throughout its existence, the Congressional Science and Engineering Fellowship Program has been pressed to evaluate its contributions and successes. From a practical standpoint, the professional societies, private foundations, and corporate offices that financed the various constituent fellowship programs wanted to know if their expenditures were worthwhile. For all parties concerned, after all, the enterprise was an appendage to their mainstream efforts. On an administrative level, recruitment of well-qualified applicants and solicitations of congressional placements for future Fellows also depended upon continued positive assessments of the program.

The criteria for success, however, were not necessarily the same for all the participants. Nor did the criteria necessarily remain fixed over time. The performance of the program depended, in part, on what aspect or aspects one was evaluating. The contributions of the fellowship program could be viewed from various angles: benefits to the users of the Fellows (that is, to the congressional members, committees, and subcommittees); benefits to the Fellows themselves; benefits to the sponsoring organizations; and benefits to the society at large. This chapter explores some of the impacts of the collaborative enterprise on the principal participating groups.

The Users of Science and Engineering Fellows

The appeal of science and engineering Fellows to congressional members and their staffs varied widely, depending upon the mix of personalities and circumstances. But one practical element always remained paramount: providing free, professional assistance. The workload for congressional offices was virtually limitless, yet every office operated under a finite budget. In his end-of-the-year report, charter Fellow Elliot Segal remarked that, although he failed to appreciate it at the time, "the orientation interviewing is about the only period when congressmen, and particularly their staffs, will be trying to sell you. They are so desperately understaffed that an intelligent body who can come free is a valuable commodity."[1] The advantage of bringing their own salaries with them was complemented by the fact that most Fellows posed little threat to the regular staff: everyone knew their terms ended in 12 months. These two circumstances worked in favor of the Fellows fitting in well.

There were, of course, nonremunerative costs associated with hosting a congressional Fellow. As newcomers to the legislative branch, Fellows had much to learn about their new assignments, and the orientation, training, and supervision of Fellows necessarily required time on the part of one or more members of the regular staff. Depending on the Fellow and the circumstances within the host office, it might be two or three months after taking on a Fellow before the office saw a net increase in overall staff productivity. Some offices were willing to make this investment; others were not, especially with the likelihood that the Fellow would soon be leaving.[2] Indiana Representative Lee H. Hamilton spoke to this concern in a letter that—on all other accounts—praised the American Philosophical Association's (APA) congressional fellowship program. Hamilton told APA that it would be helpful if its Fellows could remain with Congress for over a year. "The reasons for the suggestion are two," he said. "First, I have found that a significant amount of time (at least a month, in most cases) is spent orienting a fellow to Congress and helping him get a grip on the institution. The time spent by the fellow on legislative work is correspondingly reduced. Second, a fellow improves as he gains experience in Congress. I could take better advantage of that experience if his tenure with me were extended."[3]

Benjamin Cooper, an American Physical Society congressional Fellow in the first year group, observed in 1974 that by providing extra staff members that would otherwise not be there, the science and engineering Fellows Allowed a congressional office "to expand its capabilities into areas . . . which could not be covered with existing staff." For committees in particular, he thought this paid important dividends for the legislative process. "Congress generally hopes to avoid a situation in which the 'staff runs the show,' and this inclination mitigates against the development of a large, strong staff," he said with regard to office politics on Capitol Hill. "Yet the complexity of the issues the Congress faces and the strength of the Executive Branch and special interest lobbies require strong, flexible Congressional staff support. The need to organize these efforts without creating a staff bureaucracy that unduly influences policy decisions will emerge as an important issue in the future. To some extent the Congressional Fellowships help to underline the development of this issue."[4]

Jerome Paul Harper, an engineer who split his 1974-75 fellowship between the Office of Technology Assessment (OTA) and the personal office of Michigan Senator Philip Hart, expressed sentiments shared by many of his colleagues. The real impact of the science and engineering fellowship program "was not so much in the addition of an informed viewpoint as in the introduction of a different perspective." He claimed that "the issues raised and questions asked by an engineer or scientist are different from those asked by the lawyer-type staffer who dominates the Congressional scene."[5]

With more than 500 Fellows placed within the Congress during the first two decades, the direct beneficiaries of the program—that is, the offices of individual members and the various committees and subcommittees that have hosted one or more science and engineering Fellows—have had a broad array of rewards and experiences, most good but some bad. Occasionally, Fellows would begin assignments and soon discover that they were predisposed to either dislike or find unfulfilling the generally anonymous work of a congressional staffer. A few Fellows found themselves in offices where staff leadership did not take advantage of their skills and knowledge, perhaps relegating them solely to mundane assignments as though they were college interns. When such mismatches occurred, the AAAS staff intervened (if asked) to help rectify the situation or, on the rare occasion where it seemed the best option, to encourage the Fellow to find a placement in another office.[6]

Although the specific circumstances surrounding each fellowship assignment were to some extent unique, certain overarching patterns did emerge. For example, a few congressional members such as George E. Brown and Albert Gore, Jr., had outstanding success in welcoming Fellows into their offices.[7] Not unexpectedly, the House Committee on Science, Space, and Technology was one of the heaviest utilizers of Fellows. John D. Holmfeld, who began his 20-year career with the committee in 1971, said the professional staff recognized from the beginning that in order to take full advantage of the fellowship program, the Fellows would have to be treated as though they were regular staff members. And such was the case for the dozens of Fellows who landed assignments with the committee during the program's first two decades.[8]

Responsibilities handed Fellows working for the House Science Committee were often quite substantial. Michael R. Rubin, the American Society of Mechanical Engineers (ASME) Congressional Fellow for 1990, is a case in point. Rubin worked for the Subcommittee on Transportation, Aviation, and Materials, assisting the Republican vice chairman, Tom Lewis. As the Florida representative recalled at the end of Rubin's fellowship, "Mike had the lead Republican staff responsibility for 19 hearings and numerous legislative initiatives. In my experience, that is an unprecedented level of responsibility for a congressional fellow. Moreover, the technical background memos and suggested questions on each hearing were very accurate and extremely helpful."[9] Thomas H. Althuis, the ACS-sponsored Fellow in 1978-79 who served with the Subcommittee on Science, Research, and Technology, enjoyed a similar range of responsibilities. An expert in the development of antiallergy drugs, he was asked to monitor the General Accounting Office investigation of the Food and Drug Administration's approval process for new drugs. That assignment involved full preparation of hearings on that topic. This meant, in the words of reporter David Hanson, "outlining objectives for the hearings, interviewing and selecting witnesses, contacting the news media and writing press releases, preparing briefings for subcommittee members, and writing opening remarks for the cochairmen."[10]

Ezra Heitowit, who was staff director of the House Subcommittee on Science, Research, and Technology during the early 1980s, recalled that he and his colleagues were eager to attract Fellows to the office. Although there were some exceptions, he said they generally gave Fellows assignments associated with hearings and oversight responsibilities, as opposed to developing legislation, which required more extensive experience. Heitowit said that aside from the services they rendered, he was also motivated to host Fellows because of the long-term societal benefits to be derived from those participants who later went on to jobs in universities, industry, government agencies, nongovernment organizations, and the like, taking with them a firsthand knowledge of how the legislative branch works.[11]

In evaluating what difference the Congressional Science and Engineering Fellowship program made, it is important to consider the needs of the Congress. Generally speaking, congressional members do not need technical information such as the atomic weight of gold or the melting point of iron; they need staff members who are comfortable dealing with science and technology-related policy issues. Because of an often unspoken aversion to science and engineering among many staff members, the general scientific and technical literacy of the Fellows proved extremely useful. The Fellows offered congressional offices the ability to evaluate, probe, question, and translate technical materials; they also knew where to look for technical information or second opinions when the need arose.

Haven Whiteside addressed this issue in his 1975 end-of-the-year fellowship report to the American Physical Society. "One question that I am frequently asked shows a misunderstanding of the possible role of a physicist on Capitol Hill," he wrote.

> I am not a technical expert or a consultant on any particular issue: the interests of the [Senate] Committee [on

Environment and Public Works] are so wide ranging it would be impossible to be expert in more than one issue out of hundreds. Therefore, I must be considered as a generalist who has a particular background and training as a scientist, in particular as a physicist. This provides me with some facility for working with numbers, graphs and tables, the tools of our scientific trade. It also allows me some facility in talking with other scientific and technical people in the Administration and outside of government as well. Using these "communication skills," my job is to get information from sources into a form usable by the committee staff and members and likewise to get legislative information back to those who are interested outside of the Congress. This of course requires the writing of reports. These tend to be short: three to five pages would be long. They summarize a particular event or document and are used as the basis for our briefing books and discussing the issues. Thus, in a word, the job is that of a communicator and I find that rather interesting.[12]

Observers of the program sometimes disagreed about the best ways to maximize the effectiveness of science and engineering Fellows. For example, Patricia Garfinkel, who has served as a speech writer for the past four chairmen of the House Committee on Science, Space, and Technology, has clear ideas of how the program might be strengthened. She contends that the congressional Fellows traditionally reap far greater benefits from the program than do the members of Congress. Fellows come to the program knowing that they will devote a year of their lives to the enterprise; and, even if they know little of the Congress and policy-making, they receive at least two weeks of orientation training from AAAS and usually approach the experience as empty vessels, learning a tremendous amount about the ins and outs of the legislative branch.

Garfinkel argues that members of Congress have a far more difficult task in that they are often unprepared for how to make full and effective use of scientifically and technically trained Fellows. Occasionally, members and their staffs use the science and engineering Fellows just as they use college interns, giving them routine tasks that fail to play to the Fellows' long suits and fail to tap their expensive training in the sciences and engineering. The problem is that legislators often do not understand the expertise they have at hand; therefore, they don't know how to take advantage of it. Garfinkel's suggestion is that AAAS, or some other body, provide an orientation training session for congressional members and staff for how they might best use the science and engineering Fellows provided them.[13]

Albert Teich of AAAS provided a mirror image of the critique posed by Garfinkel. From Teich's perspective, it was neither appropriate nor realistic to ask congressional members to change so that they might make better use of science and engineering Fellows. He believed the burden should be placed on the other side: it was incumbent on AAAS and other participating societies to make the Fellows more useful to Congress.[14] Teich and Garfinkel agreed that the program could be improved, but they each placed the major responsibility for change upon their own institution.

Perspectives that Garfinkel and Teich raised rarely found expression in the words of congressional members, who tended to list different reasons for wanting to sponsor a science and engineering Fellow. However, the reasons usually involved that special technical expertise associated with the Fellows. "It is often frustrating for a member of Congress to try to develop scientific resources for legislative action," said Representative Fred Richmond of New York in support of the Fellows program. "The Library of Congress' staff is both qualified and helpful, but has an incredible burden of work which reduces the time and resources available to any single Member. The Committee Staff is also helpful, but it owes its allegiance to committee members first."[15]

Freshman Senator Dale Bumpers of Arkansas recruited AAAS Congressional Fellow William R. Moomaw to his personal staff in 1976. Bumpers, who had worked with other technically trained staff members when he was governor of Arkansas, saw the Congressional Science and Engineering Fellowship Program as a means to strengthen his effectiveness in his committee assignments with Interior and Aeronautical and Space Sciences. The latter assignment, in particular, attracted Bumpers, as he sought and won the chairmanship of the Ad Hoc Subcommittee on the Upper Atmosphere. Moomaw, who held a doctorate in physical chemistry from MIT, eventually gained extensive staff responsibilities in dealing with the subcommittee's initiatives in addressing the ozone depletion issue.[16]

Committees and subcommittees with ongoing responsibilities associated with science and engineering had obvious interests in acquiring technically trained Fellows. Often, members of Congress expressed a desire to sponsor a Fellow, citing their committee and subcommittee assignments as the principal need for such expert assistance. Individual representatives and senators also sought Fellows to assist them with concerns more focused on their congressional district or state. Such concerns tended to address issues related to health, energy, and the environment. For example, Representative Cecil Heftel of Hawaii said he shared "the concerns of many public officials regarding the accuracy, or lack thereof, of information upon which we base our energy policies. Often legislators must rely on information from the energy industry in formulating policies to meet our energy needs and demands." In his opinion, science and engineering Fellows could help reduce that dependence.[17]

Environmental concerns motivated New York Representative John J. LaFalce to seek a science and engineering Fellow in 1980. His congressional district encompassed Love Canal, the hazardous waste dump site in upstate New York that LaFalce described as "one of the most tragic and distressing environmental problems in the nation." Recent discovery of this deadly environmental health hazard had thrust LaFalce's office into the role of dealing with legislation and regulations associated with the "environmental problems caused by industrial wastes of all kinds." In addition to his concerns about Love Canal, the hundreds of other hazardous waste dump sites in his district, and the thousands of others around the country, he was also engaged with the policy implications of addressing the nation's nuclear waste sites. "Within my District, in fact only a few miles from the Love Canal, is the 'Lake Ontario Ordnance Works' site," he wrote. "Stored there is about 90 percent of the wastes from the Manhattan Project—some 20,000 tons of primarily low-level radioactive wastes, including half of the world's known supply of radium. Understandably, existence of this site has caused concerns in the minds of neighboring communities and has led my office into very detailed work on how to deal with this particular situation as well as how to deal with nuclear waste generally."[18]

Representative Robert L. Livingston, from Louisiana's 1st District, also sought to attract a science and engineering Fellow to his office to assist with a pressing environmental problem for his constituents. "Louisiana is sinking at a rate of more than 60 square miles annually," he noted to the incoming fellowship class of 1982. "In addition, thousands of acres of cypress and fresh water wetlands are being lost to salt water intrusion. One of the parishes in my district could disappear in the next 50 years." He sought a Fellow willing to research this environmental problem and to propose legislative and regulatory solutions.[19]

Many members of Congress were not predisposed to host science and engineering Fellows, often because they had had little firsthand experience working closely with technically trained professionals. Of course, providing such experience was one of the original driving motivations behind creating the fellowship program, and winning converts to seeing the advantages of adding scientists and engineers to their regular staffs was deemed a sign of success by AAAS and its sister organizations.

Representative Al Swift of Washington fitted squarely in this category of converts, as he became strongly committed to the science and engineering fellowship program following his experience in sponsoring the American Geophysical Union's (AGU) 1981-82 Fellow, George H. Shaw. "I must admit I was skeptical as to the value of having a scientist in the office for a year, a skepticism which I suspect would likely be shared by most members of Congress who tend to be steeped in the humanities or, worse, the law," Swift wrote to AGU's executive director. "That skepticism, I think, grows out of a prejudice: that scientists are both too clinical and too 'ivory tower' to function well in the visceral and rough and tumble world of political policy making." Following his year working with Shaw, Swift reported: "Today, I know that is pure bunk."

> I am very glad that I "hired" a science fellow. I've learned many things about science and scientists and have

a much better appreciation for the significant potential impact of science and technology on public policy.

Further, I am now convinced of the need for more technically trained people in the congressional legislative process. While the committee staffs often boast very capable scientists, it is extremely rare to find technically or scientifically trained people on the personal staffs of members who, in fact, deal with technical issues all the time. Because Congressional staff work like graduate school involves long hours, lots of work, and low pay, the individual Member of Congress seldom has the ability to hire people with a matured scientific background. This is unfortunate and the process suffers for it.

However, in addition to being a member of the House Energy and Commerce Committee which deals with many technical issues all the time, I'm a member of the House Administration Committee. In that capacity I will have a chance to raise the issue of staffing in Congressional offices as it relates to the need for technically trained staff. I imagine that, to date, relatively few members realize the degree to which staff members with a science or technical background could improve the overall effectiveness of their offices.

The Science Fellows Program serves a very useful purpose in making Members of Congress more aware of the contributions scientists can make in the legislative process. Beyond that, it also serves to demonstrate that scientists, just like lawyers, journalists, businessmen, farmers and all the rest can function very effectively in a political arena.[20]

One measure of the effectiveness of the fellowship program was the length to which many congressional members and staff went to attract new Fellows. For example, Albert Gore, Jr., both as a representative and later as a senator, with great conviction solicited potential Fellows. In summer 1978, Gore expressed his "very deep interest in having an AAAS Fellow" serve in his office, preferably one interested in rural health problems, which Gore intended to address in the forthcoming year. "I could offer a health fellow a challenging opportunity to utilize his or her health expertise and political skills," he wrote. "I feel confident that a Fellow could make significant progress in a year in developing a comprehensive health care delivery system. I would work closely with the Fellow and could offer guidance in gaining access to the appropriate health officials."[21] In an attempt to increase the appeal of his office, Gore emphasized the manner in which he worked with Fellows: "I like to leave the duties and responsibilities of a Fellow as flexible as possible in order to maximize their input into day-to-day matters. I can assure you that I would develop a close working relationship with the Fellow because I work best when I am totally involved in an issue and understand every nuance as well as my staff."[22]

California Representative George E. Brown, who has provided assignments to more science and engineering Fellows than anyone else in Congress, went out of his way to recruit Fellows from the beginning of the program. Brown's 1977 letter to the upcoming Fellows class was typical of those efforts. "My basic practice is to have the Fellow become a full member of what I hope is a fairly stimulating kind of staff organization—one in which information flows freely in nonhierarchal ways and in which the staff and I interact informally in 'floating' groups addressed to issues of concern to all of us," he stated. "I do try to give the Fellows the freedom to concentrate on their areas of special skill and interest and avoid having them bogged down with some of the routine of our office function. Last, I feel strongly that the year should be a genuine learning process for the Fellows, so I encourage them to design their work with that in mind."[23]

Brown's administrative assistant, Skip Stiles, encouraged the 1983 class of Fellows to consider assignments on Brown's staff. Praising the high quality of the former Fellows with which they had worked, he stated that "we have always valued their contribution to our office."[24] Three years later, Brown praised the fellowship program and its residual benefits to AAAS's Stephen Nelson, telling him that "it is getting so that I cannot deal with a federal agency, scientific society, or research institution without running into a former Fellow."[25]

Michigan Representative Howard Wolpe had also enjoyed mutually beneficial relations with former Fellows and looked forward to drawing future Fellows to his office. "We have always made fellows a regular part of our legislative staff," he said in offering his office as a future fellowship assignment. "Participants would be responsible for maintaining their legislative portfolio, preparing my floor packet for their areas, drafting speeches and floor statements, responding to constituent correspondence, and conducting research on specialized topics of interest to me and him or her." He added that "the only *absolute requirement*" for a Congressional fellow was a sense of humor, as "no one would survive here without one!"[26]

Senator Jeff Bingaman of New Mexico wrote in a similar vein in his 1984 attempt to lure another Fellow. Bingaman described his delight in the work of American Physical Society Fellow Tony Fainberg, who was just completing his fellowship year. Fainberg "has worked on projects as diverse as expanded use of polygraphs in the Defense Department, trying to spur university-national laboratory-industry cooperation in R&D in New Mexico, verification of arms control agreements limiting nuclear explosive testing, nuclear waste disposal at the Waste Isolation Pilot Plant in New Mexico, military construction in Central America, anti-satellite arms control, and defense procurement reform," Bingaman said. "In the past three months he has been handling foreign affairs since an American Political Science Association Fellow left my office."[27]

To the extent that Congress operates in a reactive fashion to trends and events, the opportunities presented each year's class of Fellows were in part molded by the most pressing concerns of the moment. The Arab oil embargo, the breakup of the Atomic Energy Commission, the Clinch River Breeder Reactor, Three Mile Island, acid rain, endangered species, wetlands regulation, depletion of the ozone layer, global warming, ocean dumping, the Space Shuttle, Skylab, the Superconducting Super Collider, biotechnology regulation, the Women's Health Initiative, AIDS research, information policy, technology trade agreements, the Strategic Defense Initiative, and the Persian Gulf War all prompted congressional responses that often involved oversight, authorization, and appropriations, which in turn presented short-term needs that science and engineering Fellows were often able to fill in meaningful and productive ways.

Issues related to energy and the environment continued to occupy the talents of the majority of science and engineering Fellows in the 1980s, just as they had done during the 1970s. The dominance of energy and environmental policy concerns was slightly lessened, however, by the expansion of the participating societies, which brought to the congressional fellowship program health scientists, social scientists, and humanists who were drawn to other concerns. Physical scientists and engineers also found an expanded range of fellowship opportunities as the scope of public policy concerns that explicitly contained elements of science and technology broadened. Washington Senator Slade Gorton pointed to this fact in commending the fellowship program on its 10th anniversary in 1983. Gorton told his Senate colleagues that "in light of the increasingly technological character of many of the critical issues before us, the congressional science and engineering fellows program may be even more timely now than at its beginning."[28]

Pointing to an example of the needs created by high-profile events, Radford Byerly, staff director of the House Subcommittee on Space Science and Applications in 1986, expressed his desire for Fellows: "I believe we can offer a particularly interesting experience in the coming year because the Challenger accident is forcing a fundamental review of U.S. space policy. Our Subcommittee on Space Science and Applications is and will be in the middle of the debate."[29] The esteem Byerly held for the science and engineering fellowship program was shared by several congressional reform groups, perhaps none more enthusiastic than the Carnegie Commission on Science, Technology, and Government, which issued a widely disseminated report in 1991 calling for the fellowship program to be strengthened and expanded.[30]

Personal Experiences

It would be misleading to claim that there was a typical experience among science and engineering Fellows, or that all the fellowships were successful. The variety was immense; no doubt there have been as many experiences as there have been Fellows—more than 500 through the first 20 years. So, too, did the motivations for wanting to serve as a congressional Fellow vary widely among the applicants. For most participants, the fellowship added something special and unusual to their professional lives, and as such often opened up postfellowship employment and career options that otherwise would not have existed. Some pursued these new opportunities; others did not.

"Potomac Fever," a disease whose main symptom is an addiction to Washington's seductive atmosphere of politics and power, is spread most easily among those who find themselves working on the inside of government policy-making. A congressional fellowship was not in itself a necessarily powerful or prestigious position, but it placed its holders ever so close to some of the nation's principal power brokers, and as such tempted many a Fellow to stay in Washington—if not with the Congress, then with some other organization within or relating to the federal government.

The first class of Fellows faced career choices that were repeated among many of those who followed. For example, American Physical Society Fellow Richard Werthamer chose not to pursue a career in government service for family reasons and the financial sacrifice it would have entailed. "I looked to the Fellowship experience more for a wide exposure to a range of issues on which technology and government interact, and to the mechanisms by which that interaction takes place," he said, "than as a training for a new career in government." He decided to return to his previous post at Bell Laboratories, while seeking opportunities within the company for "a new role as a scientist with a knowledge of government; a scientist who works actively to bring the scientific profession more into contact with, and more at the service of, government and its dealings with national issues."[31] Werthamer later left Bell Laboratories to devote more of his time to science policy issues, eventually becoming executive secretary of the American Physical Society in New York City.

Benjamin Cooper, also an American Physical Society Fellow, followed a different course of action, accepting an offer as a professional staff member with the Senate Interior and Insular Affairs Committee, where he had spent his fellowship. Cooper explained that staying with the Congress meant giving up his tenured faculty appointment at Iowa State University. "All over the country tenured positions in physics departments are filling up," he wrote at the end of his fellowship year, "and they will remain full for at least a generation. Turning down that position to stay in Washington meant foreclosing any possibility of a job as a physics professor in the future."[32] Twenty years later, Cooper remains with the same Senate committee—its name changed to the Committee on Energy and Natural Resources in 1977—having risen to become staff director.

Institute of Electrical and Electronics Engineers (IEEE) Congressional Fellow Ronal Larson had gained substantial insight into proposed solar energy legislation in his work for the House Committee on Science and Astronautics' Energy Subcommittee; he decided to apply that knowledge at the Office of Technology Assessment, where he accepted a one-year position as project director of the Solar Power Production Assessment, one of the first major assessments undertaken by the office.[33]

At the conclusion of his fellowship year with Senator Warren Magnuson of Washington, AAAS Congressional Fellow Elliot Segal was torn about which direction to head. "The choices of future career directions for me is [sic] currently quite hazy. Many options are now open to me, and I have not yet been able to resolve the internal desires I now have to move in several directions at once," wrote the former Yale University School of Medicine assistant dean in 1974. "I have considered offers as a legislative assistant (in Senator Magnuson's office), as an administrator-planner with HEW-Assistant Secretary for Health, as a staff person for a new Presidential Commission on the future of biomedical research, and as a Team Director for a Congressional Study for the Institute of Medicine. I am quite sure none of these options would have been available to me had I not been a fellow."[34]

First-year Fellow Michael Telson, who came into the program as a freshly minted Ph.D., also faced an enticing array of career choices at the end of his fellowship year. Telson had concentrated on energy-related issues at the Senate Interior and Insular Affairs Committee, and this experience led to job offers at the Council on Environmental Quality, Environmental Protection Agency, Federal Energy Administration, and National Science Foundation, as well as offers from two private companies and three universities. "However," he confessed, "at the time I felt my career goals would best be served by remaining on the Hill in a position from which I could delve into energy, economic, and environmental issues."[35] Telson recalled how the frantic pace of the fellowship year left him with a feeling of frustration and incompleteness; he wanted to stay with Congress for another two or three years to help bring to fruition some of the legislative initiatives that had occupied his time as a Fellow. He found such an opportunity in December 1974 when the newly created House Budget Committee hired him as the professional staff member responsible for energy and the environment. The two or three years he planned to work for Congress soon became 10 years and then 20, as Telson has remained on the Budget Committee staff, where he is a senior analyst with responsibilities for energy, science, and space.[36]

For the science and engineering Fellows who decided not to return to their former jobs or type of employment, the fellowship experience most certainly proved a catalytic element in those decisions, but rarely was it the sole factor in such moves. Indeed, the decision to apply for the congressional fellowship itself involved a self-selecting process, as the program attracted candidates who, for one reason or another, were willing to remove themselves from their routines of research, teaching, or industrial employment to play a part in the legislative process. Many of these Fellows had already been engaged in activities associated with the intersection of society with science and technology. Allan Hoffman, an APS congressional Fellow in 1974-75, exemplified such a situation.

Hoffman had been a member of the physics department at the University of Massachusetts before spending his fellowship year with the Senate Committee on Commerce, Science, and Transportation. When the committee offered him a staff position at the end of his fellowship, Hoffman accepted. "My commitment to public service science activities began to build several years before I received the fellowship," he explained in 1975, "and I was gradually shifting my academic teaching, research, and service activities in response to this growing interest." The fellowship answered any doubts he had about whether he would find government service rewarding. Nevertheless, he remained torn about his decision, knowing that "staying in Washington meant giving up the perquisites of academic life for at least a while, and perhaps indefinitely. It meant giving up a chance to teach, to do research on solar and other energy systems, and to shape graduate and undergraduate environmental education programs." The uncertainties did not dissuade him from pursuing a new career, but as he confessed: "Staying in Washington means no return to a conventional physics career . . . staying in Washington is a gamble, but one I'm willing to make because of the new and interesting opportunities that will hopefully be open to me . . ."[37]

Hoffman has remained an active player in the Washington science policy community. Following his fellowship, he stayed on with the Senate Commerce Committee for a year and a half before joining the Department of Energy. In 1982, he moved to the National Academy of Sciences, where he served for eight years as executive director of the Committee on Science, Engineering, and Public Policy. In 1990, he returned to the Department of Energy, where he now holds the title of associate deputy assistant secretary for utility technology within the Office of Conservation and Renewable Energy.[38]

Lloyd B. Craine, the 1974-75 IEEE Fellow, returned to his tenured professorship in electrical engineering at Washington State University, despite his deeply satisfying and stimulating year with the House Committee on Science and Technology. He wrote that the fellowship gave him "an opportunity to provide a public service to the Congress and to learn a great deal about the actual operation of the Political World. I will be able to integrate this experience into my teaching of new engineers and, through continuing activities with IEEE, will help to make this fellowship year an experience of value to many persons."[39]

Like Craine, Haven Whiteside came to the 1974-75 congressional fellowship as a tenured professor. However, Whiteside decided his American Physical Society fellowship was not long enough, and when the Senate Committee on Environment and Public Works offered him a staff position, he accepted. He hedged his bets, however, by securing another year's leave of absence from the physics department at Federal City College in Washington, D.C., saying that he found "himself attracted to the college community and it would be interesting to go back and try to bring questions of public policy into college science education." Nevertheless, he thought it important in his final report to address a criticism that was starting to be expressed about the two-year-old fellowship program:

> The suggestion has been made that perhaps too many of the Fellows are staying on and not enough going back to academia. I cannot believe this is true as yet. There are many offices and many committees on Capitol Hill, and most of them are staffed with people trained in law and political science. It seems to me that most offices could use at least one person with a scientific background. My hope would be that new Fellows from the Physical Society and other societies will spread themselves among many different offices rather than concentrating on the few with the most science responsibilities. If we do become adequately spread, a scientific way of thinking will be present, at least as a background, in most of the key committees. Then we might speak of some saturation, but we have not reached that stage yet.[40]

William R. Moomaw held a tenured professorship in chemistry at Williams College when he took leave in 1975-76 to accept an AAAS congressional fellowship. Although he returned to Williams at the close of his year working for Senator Dale Bumpers, Moomaw continued to serve the Arkansas senator as a part-time legislative assistant to work on legislative issues that had been his earlier responsibility. Moomaw stressed in his final report that his scientific training proved enormously important in his work on ozone depletion issues, yet ultimately he thought that "all of that technical background would have been of little use had I not been able to interact with and mesh smoothly with other non-technically trained staff people, lobbyists, and indeed, Senator Bumpers himself." Moomaw also expressed a reaction to "the anonymity of a staff person," a view shared by many Fellows. He wrote:

> As a scientist one publishes his work, puts his name on it, and then waits to receive either his lumps or his praise. It is very strange therefore to see one's words (and even stranger to hear them) credited to someone else. I wrote a number of floor statements, speeches, and individual views in committee reports for Senator Bumpers. In fact, I probably "published" more this year than at any other time in my

life. But writing for someone else in the first person, taking into account his viewpoints and political sensibilities, is a peculiar experience.[41]

Robert H. Barker, American Chemical Society Fellow for 1981-82, proved to be the right person at the right place at the right time. He was the J.E. Sirrine Professor of Textile and Polymer Chemistry at Clemson University before his fellowship. He chose to spend his year with freshman Representative Judd Gregg from New Hampshire. Barker was Gregg's only staff member with scientific training. Because the congressman was assigned to the Committee on Government Operations' Subcommittee on Environment, Energy, and Natural Resources and the Committee on Science and Technology's Subcommittee on Energy Development and Applications and Subcommittee on Science, Research, and Technology, Barker spent much of his time attending to legislative matters pertaining to those subcommittees. Such matters included acid rain, nuclear waste disposal, patent policy, science education, and the treatment of research animals. Gregg quickly came to rely on Barker's judgment and abilities. After three months, Gregg appointed Barker legislative director. Following his fellowship year, Barker remained on staff, working as Gregg's administrative assistant and maintaining an adjunct position with Clemson University. The fellowship year not only changed Barker's allocation of time after the fellowship, but also changed his teaching. He was inspired to develop a new course at Clemson on technology and public policy.[42]

Norine E. Noonan, an ACS Fellow in 1982-83, came to the program from Georgetown University. She arranged an assignment with the Senate Committee on Commerce, Science, and Transportation's Subcommittee on Science, Technology, and Space. Following her fellowship, she went to work for the Office of Management and Budget, addressing budgetary issues relating to science and technology. Writing to her chemistry colleagues about the ACS congressional fellowship program, Noonan stated:

> It's not what you expect; you don't do fancy things. You think you're going to walk in and write legislation, and it doesn't happen. It's not exactly "Mr. Smith Goes to Washington."

During the waning days of the 97th Congress, Harrison Schmitt, chairman of the Senate Subcommittee on Science, Technology, and Space, was asked to contribute to an issue of the journal, *Technology in Society*. He asked me to write the article, which dealt with a history of congressional action in the recombinant DNA controversy as well as the role of Congress in biotechnology today.

When you are a staff person to a representative or senator, you are expected to be anonymous. It's frustrating for scientists who are used to being principal authors. It's tough to live with if you can never put your name on anything. However, the fun of crafting that article and the special thanks of Senator Schmitt were more than adequate recompense.[43]

The question of anonymity rubbed several Fellows the wrong way. Paul Horwitz, the 1975-76 American Physical Society congressional Fellow, described his year on the staff of Massachusetts Senator Edward M. Kennedy as wonderfully exhilarating and fulfilling, save for the expectation that staff members forever remain in the shadows. There was something "that bothered me about the role of legislative aide, something I hadn't anticipated, and that no one had warned me about," he wrote in his year-end evaluation. "In fact, I was surprised to discover that it bothered me at all, yet I suspect that most scientists would feel the same way. It was the *anonymity* of my position that got to me." He went on to describe this situation for the benefit of future Fellows:

> Scientists place great store in public recognition. It is important to them that their work receive the attention of their peers, and that their personal contributions be publicly acknowledged. Pride of authorship runs deep in the scientific community, where the charge of "idea stealing" is the equivalent of horse thievery in the old West.
>
> But a legislative aide's job requires anonymity. He may spend three weeks drafting a major address on foreign policy, but it is not and cannot ever be his speech. His boss will stand up in front of the cheering crowd to deliver it while he sits nervously and obscurely in a back row, anticipating each phrase as it appears, relaxing when the

jokes bring a laugh, flinching as the name of an African prime minister is mispronounced, and applauding like a madman when it is all over. And the *Times* may hail it the next morning as a major step forward, but his name will never be mentioned. Call it vanity or *hubris*—I could never accept such a low profile on a permanent basis.[44]

The reflections of Thomas Althuis, a 1978-79 American Chemical Society (ACS) Fellow, were shared by many of his colleagues. "It is extremely important and beneficial for scientists to get themselves involved in government," he said. "It helps show them how to get scientific ideas across to government and helps point out the overall pictures to legislators who do not have time for many details. Such involvement will help scientists as a group to exert influence on the decisions made by government."[45] That last remark—that interactions like those associated with the Fellows program will amplify the scientific community's voice within the arena of government decision making—was at once narrow and self-serving. Yet it nevertheless remained a motivation (albeit usually unspoken) for the scientific societies' continued sponsorship of the Fellows program. As such, it seemed to run counter to the stated and implied objectives of service to society, but such conflicting motives have been an indelible part of human nature.

Such sentiments were expressed by Stephen Ziman, an industrial chemist who served as one of two ACS Fellows in 1979-80. Ziman's year on the Hill convinced him that chemists needed to become more aggressive and vocal in their defense of chemistry. "We need to do a little consciousness-raising about chemistry and science at the federal level," he advised his ACS colleagues.[46] John Wiesenfeld, chairman of the ACS Committee on Chemistry and Public Affairs in 1991, told the society's membership that the congressional Fellows program not only offers "a unique personal growth opportunity for the fellow, but it is also a real opportunity for ACS to establish a scientific presence in Congress."[47]

Sometimes the congressional fellowship affected the participants in unexpected ways; other times its effects were quite predictable. Gerald L. Epstein, one of the 1983-84 Office of Technology Assessment (OTA) Fellows, fit the latter category. "Midway through my Ph.D. program at Berkeley," Epstein wrote at the end of the fellowship, "I had seriously considered leaving the physics department for one of the interdisciplinary science and public policy programs that are now appearing on a number of campuses. I finally decided to go ahead and get the physics degree and see what I could do in policy afterwards." He found the OTA fellowship a superb way to make the transition. "The fellowship is the ideal mechanism for a person with a science background to get into technology assessment and policy analysis. Although it is certainly possible to make such a transition without the fellowship (and I submit there would never have been a fellowship program had not some people previously made that transition successfully on their own), having the fellowship has made that career path much more tenable."[48] Epstein found his fellowship experience so satisfying that he accepted an offer as a regular analyst with OTA and has remained there ever since.

Occasionally, unanticipated events catapulted an already invigorating year into something quite remarkable. For example, Missouri Representative Richard A. Gephardt's decision to run for the presidency in 1986 swept up the lives of at least one current and one former science and engineering Fellow. Alice V. Zeiger, an ACS Fellow for 1986-87, found her "routine" shattered when, halfway through her fellowship, Gephardt announced his candidacy. Given her expertise in environmental chemistry as it related to public health, Zeiger assisted in monitoring health policy issues for Gephardt and helped write speeches on AIDS.[49] Andrea B. King, an American Philosophical Association Fellow who had remained in her staff position after her 1984-85 fellowship, was also affected by Gephardt's presidential run.

Cheryl G. Tropf, in summing up her first months as a 1980-81 American Mathematical Society/Mathematical Association of America/Society for Industrial and Applied Mathematics Fellow with the Senate Committee on Commerce, Science, and Transportation, expressed a rather common perception of the Fellows. "The work that I am doing—meetings, issue papers, hearings, etc.—has very little to do with mathematical research—no one knows what a differential equation is, much less asks you to solve it," she confessed. "Much of the work can be described as being in the broad area of science policy, which I think is a natural progression for a person to follow along a career path in science. So far, I haven't missed doing basic mathematics, but I do feel that I could return to it."[50]

Anne Harris Cohn, a 1978-79 Society for Research in Child Development Congressional Fellow, spoke to another concern. "I had learned that some academics regard the Congressional Science Fellowship as an unfortunate career disruption," she said, "as irrelevant as an unexcused absence when former Fellows are considered for academic posts. A friend of mine who had just finished a fellowship in Washington, D.C., said she was returning to her university with a fair amount of trepidation. 'They just don't understand why I wanted to spend a year with the government,' she explained. 'It will take months for me to reestablish my credentials with my colleagues as a serious researcher. And with some, I may never do so.'" Dismayed by this reaction, Cohn told her colleagues there are three basic reasons that underpin the importance of the fellowship program: "First, science should be applied to social needs. Second, scientists have a responsibility in making sure that this happens. And third, scientists have a great deal to learn and understand about the policy process and applying science to social needs."[51]

Cohn went on to outline one of the basic contributions of science and engineering Fellows, saying that it is not specific technical knowledge that is important, but the scientific and technical training and approach. "The application of the scientific method becomes a valuable tool in the work of the Congress in analyzing budgets, in planning congressional investigations, in interpreting the numerous tables, charts and other forms of statistics which cross a Congressman's desk," she insisted. "Knowing not only when to question the validity of information but also how to question it becomes a valuable function that the Fellow can serve. The Fellow, because of his or her special training, brings to a congressional staff the facility for communicating with the technical and scientific world."[52] Grant Carrow had another way of expressing this situation. After spending 1990-91 with the Senate Committee on Labor and Human Resources, the AAAS Congressional Fellow declared: "While my [biomedical] science background was used, the depth of understanding needed here is much shallower than in Academia, and on the Hill, science takes a back seat to politics."[53]

Privately, Anne Harris Cohn spoke of her fellowship experience in her final report to AAAS. She had accepted a position on the personal staff of Tennessee Representative Albert Gore, Jr., who had expressed his interest in sponsoring a Fellow to work on health-related issues. Although Cohn spent some of her time working directly in areas of her technical specialty—public health with an emphasis on children's health—she found her major assignment pushing her beyond her specific training and experience. Upon learning that Gore wanted her to be the lead staff person for the oversight hearings on the Love Canal chemical waste problems and on the chemical waste disposal practices of the chemical industry as a whole, which were to take part over the entire year, Cohn panicked internally. "True, my doctorate was in public health—and this is a public health problem—but my specialties are health planning and children's health care programs, not toxicology or environmental health," she wrote. Nevertheless, she carried through with her assignment as best she could, noting:

> My involvement with the hazardous waste issue throughout the year was, without question, the single most vital aspect of my fellowship experience. The subject matter was new to me. I was forced to stretch my mindset beyond "social health issues" and learn about new concepts, new vocabulary, an unfamiliar federal agency (the EPA) and unfamiliar interest groups (such as the chemical industry). While tremendously difficult at first, I found that I could apply my skills as an analytic thinker and problem solver to a new area of inquiry. And, by the year's end, I felt that I had very directly contributed and influenced Congressional responses to a very significant problem.[54]

During the first two decades of the fellowship program's existence, there has been a heightened awareness of the many issues facing Congress that contain essential scientific and technological elements. As a result of this recognition and the meaningful contributions made by science and engineering Fellows, the number of technically trained legislative staff has grown since the mid-1970s. Promoters of the fellowship program have viewed this in an entirely positive light. They have shifted their rationale for a continued fellowship program by noting that the need continues to outstrip the demand; that the turnover rate among congressional staff members remains high;[55] and that the number of science and technology issues confronting members of Congress continues to expand.

James E. Evans, the 1987-88 Geological Society of America congressional Fellow, addressed this ongoing need for technically trained staff assistance in his final report. Evans, who spent his year on the personal staff of Washington Representative Mike Lowry, observed:

> It is true that the congressional staff are remarkably well informed about the issues, particularly the legal aspects of scientific issues. Where the lack of scientific training becomes a problem, in my opinion, is that the staff are not always able to question the underlying assumptions given by expert testimony. For example, one hearing that I attended featured a graphic analysis of data and trends presented by an earth scientist. *If* the analysis of the data was correct, then certain conclusions seemed rather evident. The problem, as I later pointed out to the staff, was that certain aspects of the data analysis were questionable, which may invalidate the conclusions that were given. Because most scientific witnesses only have a limited amount of time (generally five minutes) to present their studies, very few take the time to candidly discuss the limitations of their data or uncertainties of analyses. As a result, scientists often project the image of being considerably more certain of their conclusions than they would care to admit, or than they would if presenting the same studies before an audience of their professional peers.
>
> The [Geological] Society [of America] should be aware that the most important independent source of geological information on Capitol Hill is from oil company lobbyists. Many of these lobbyists are well-organized and informed, and they promptly respond to requests for information or assistance. I found that one could count upon receiving factual responses to any question I asked. The

problem is that, on their own volition, lobbyists can only be expected to offer information that would support their views. I fully respect the rights and obligations of the oil companies to present their views, but I would suggest that the needs of the geological community at large are not always compatible with the needs of the oil companies.[56]

The Sponsoring Societies

If Congress and individual Fellows gained so clearly from the program, what about the sponsoring societies? Aside from the silent satisfaction of contributing toward the good of society by raising the level of informed decision making, these professional organizations enjoyed significant prestige from simply underwriting such programs, which in turn enhanced their public image. As this result suggests, however, benefits to the sponsoring societies tended to be subtle and difficult to measure. For example, one of the persistent rationales for the fellowship program was its ability to deepen the scientific and engineering communities' understanding of the legislative branch and of policy-making in general—a goal that has certainly been approached, yet one unlikely to be assessed with much precision.

At the end of the first fellowship year, Elliot Segal summarized insights he had gained working on the personal staff of Senator Warren Magnuson. What struck him most was the value of exposing congressional members and staff—many of whom came from legal backgrounds—to professionals trained in science and engineering. In his opinion, this workplace exposure went a long way toward breaking down counterproductive stereotypes. "The thought processes and disciplines taught by the scientific method provides [sic] a different perspective from those trained to seek out precedents and build upon them," he wrote. "I feel that the growth of the AAAS program and broader exposure will convince people on Capitol Hill that it is valuable to seek out scientists for staff, and this will be the best dividend that can accrue to the advancement of science."[57]

Ronal Larson, another member of the first class of Fellows, reported on benefits reaped by his sponsoring society, the Institute of Electrical and Electronics Engineers (IEEE). Even the process of recruiting Fellows offered dividends, he asserted, and recommended to IEEE that "advertising in other journals will serve a public relations function as well as attracting more candidates." More substantially, he agreed that the fellowship program must be continually justified to the institute's membership, since each and every one of the U.S. members helps support the activity. "Partly the program is to demonstrate to Congress that IEEE is concerned with Congressional activities and is anxious to help," he said. "The value of this evidence of IEEE sincerity will only be seen in future years, through requests for IEEE opinion and expert testimony. This is certainly one important method for each IEEE member to contribute to the deliberations of Congress." He explained that "Congress works largely through an informal network of contacts," and that the Fellows can help integrate electrical engineers into that system. Educating the IEEE membership about the legislative process and congressional operations was another advantage of the program. "The Congress is a surprisingly small organization with a minimum of technical input," he stated, "so that a single individual can have a disproportionately large influence on technical policy issues." He concluded that "it is of immense importance for IEEE to demonstrate its concern to Congress and to act in the national interest from a base of technical expertise."[58]

William S. Widnall, appointed in 1974 as the first American Institute of Aeronautics and Astronautics (AIAA) congressional Fellow, spent his year on Capitol Hill working on NASA-related issues for the House Committee on Science and Technology. In summing up his experience, he said that he hoped his involvement had "increased the confidence of the Members and the staff that engineers can make a valuable contribution on the Hill. Perhaps future staff openings more often will go to engineers." He also thought AIAA benefited through its expression—via the sponsorship of Fellows—of service to the Congress, which had in turn "increased the respect of the Congress for the AIAA. A benefit to the AIAA should be that when AIAA delegations visit the Hill to testify, or to visit Members and staff, such delegations will be greeted with greater trust and willingness to listen."[59]

Stephen Ziman claimed that his exposure to hearings at the House Committee on Science and Technology led him to view his sponsoring organization, the American Chemical Society (ACS), differently. "I'm much more aware of how ACS functions on the Hill," he claimed. "Of the many societies and organizations active, ACS is very well received. The testimony has had effect because it's very well thought out."[60]

From the vantage point of 1994, it is easy to see that the 500-plus former congressional science and engineering Fellows form an important resource in and of themselves. This cumulative benefit was actually recognized early in the fellowship program. At a meeting of the participating societies in 1975, those present concurred that former Fellows should be regarded as a "pool" to which they should all be encouraged to look when arranging speakers at meetings, colloquiums, and the like.[61] One year later, Richard Scribner said that one of the central responsibilities of the AAAS fellowship officers was "monitoring and keeping records of the experience and progress of the Fellows. We collect interim and final reports of all the Fellows, follow the careers of all of them after the Fellowship year, and function as a kind of alumni organization."[62]

This pool of former Fellows played numerous roles and served as a kind of "invisible college." As a group of technically trained professionals who had acquired firsthand experience on a congressional staff, these people became a resource tapped by several users: Congress itself, congressional support agencies, executive branch agencies, related science policy organizations, public interest groups, and university and corporate offices. Many former Fellows also lobbied their sponsoring societies, when necessary, to continue funding the congressional fellowship program; these Fellows became an interested constituency that pressed for this ongoing professional and social service. What political scientists Robert H. Salisbury and Kenneth A. Shepsle said about former congressional staff members as a whole certainly applies to the alumni of the Congressional Science and Engineering Fellowship Program. "In a very important sense," they argued, "the growth and turnover of congressional staff has served to provide an expanding pool of competent people to fill the myriad roles which modern public life requires. Former staffers provide a significant body of individuals who 'know the system' at a relatively complex level and can serve as guides and counselors to those who do not yet possess that competence."[63]

Pamela Ebert, a 1974-75 AAAS/American Psychological Association (APA) congressional Fellow who went to work for the National Research Council's Commission on Human Resources following her fellowship with the Senate Subcommittee on Children and Youth, exemplified this transfer of knowledge. Writing to APA in support of the program, Ebert testified: "I consider the fellowship experience to be directly related to my current role as science policy/ human resources analyst, and, in addition, to have stimulated the informal policy network which has been established, sustained, and utilized in the past year." She hoped to continue her "career in science and federal policy—a career which has been launched through the postdoctoral experience afforded by the AAAS/APA Congressional Science Fellowship Program."[64] Ebert (now Pamela Ebert Flattau) fulfilled that hope, as she has remained with the National Research Council, advancing to become director of studies and surveys for scientific and engineering personnel.

In spring 1975, Richard Scribner summarized what he thought were some of the early impacts of the science and engineering fellowship program. "There is evidence of the impact on Congress as, for example, through the Program's helping to create a greater inclination to hire scientists for staff roles within Congress," he said. "The greater visibility provided by the Program of congressionally-oriented, public-service efforts of professional scientists has, among other effects, changed for the better the attitudes of some of the members of Congress and their staffs who were previously dubious of the value of science and the utility of scientists in the legislative area."[65]

Despite whatever benefits the societies perceived that they reaped from the fellowship program, the continued funding of that effort could not be taken for granted. Not every society enjoyed large amounts of discretionary income, and financing a Fellows program had to compete with numerous other pressing and worthy projects and programs. Not only did the circumstances of the various societies range broadly, they often changed over time, causing some organizations to drop their congressional fellowship programs after several years of successful sponsorship. Champions of the congressional fellowship program either had to seek external funding or, more likely, internal funding from the society itself. The latter often involved a perennial process of reeducation of elected officials who changed periodically. This process had an unanticipated benefit of heightening the professional societies' awareness of the usefulness of engineers and scientists interacting with the government. The ongoing effort to reinvigorate support among board members of the various organizations was carried out both by the societies' paid staff and by their former congressional Fellows.[66]

Some organizations such as the American Physical Society, the American Geophysical Union, the Acoustical Society of America, the American Psychological Association, and AAAS were consistently able to support their fellowship programs through internal sources. Other societies such as the American Historical Association, the American Philosophical Association, and the Society for Research in Child Development relied on grants that, when they ceased, resulted in the termination of the program. On the other hand, the American Society for Microbiology began its fellowship program with monies received from grants, but later assumed full financial responsibility itself. Some societies split the funding through a combination of internal and external funds. For example, the Geological Society of America evenly divided the costs of its congressional fellowships with the U.S. Geological Survey. The Institute of Electrical and Electronics Engineers and the National Society for Professional Engineers relied on employers of the Fellows to pay a proportion of their stipends. Finally, some smaller societies pooled their resources to form joint ventures. These societies included: the Mathematical Association of America/American Mathematical Society/Society of Industrial and Applied Mathematics; and the American Society of Agronomy/Crop Science Society of America/Soil Science Society of America/Weed Science Society of America.[67]

Although none of the participating societies could take the funding for their fellowship programs for granted, the momentum, success, and importance of the overall effort have never really been doubted since the late 1970s. Albert H. Teich, who has held administrative oversight of the AAAS program since the early 1980s, said that commitment to the fellowship program has remained consistently high within both the scientific and engineering societies and within Congress, despite the fact that the number of scientists and engineers working for the legislative branch and its support agencies has grown substantially since the early 1970s.[68] The sustained strength of the program comes in part from the fact that the need for technically trained staff has outpaced this group's growing numbers. Conversely, the need of the scientific and engineering community for political understanding and sophistication has remained constant, as politics change and as new generations of researchers enter the profession.

Perhaps because AAAS administered the entire program—therefore receiving substantial visibility within the science, engineering, congressional, and science policy communities; and also finding the fellowship enterprise a major staff activity that helped underwrite salaries through the administrative fees paid by the participating organizations—the association's internal support base for the fellowship program never flagged after the mid-1970s. Program officers Stephen Nelson and Claudia Sturges state that, while they regularly report on the operations, status, accomplishments, and shortcomings of the fellowship program to the AAAS leadership, they have not had to defend the program's merits or utility. This unwavering support at the association's highest levels, they added, also relieved them of the need to fight for continued funding or occasional modest increases.[69] Aside from the success of the program and the above-mentioned factors, a more personal (and perhaps unmeasurable) factor was also at play: William Golden, one of the program's most steadfast supporters and the person responsible for the initial funding, has served for the last 25 years as treasurer of AAAS and a member of the board of directors. Golden's presence on the board could only help ensure the program's health. He reports, in fact, that board members have never questioned the full continuation of the enterprise.[70]

CONCLUSION

Like most institutions, the Congressional Science and Engineering Fellowship Program has not remained static. In all aspects, the program was eventually shaped by its participants, administrators, supporters, and congressional users. Changing needs and attitudes have prompted operational adjustments and the enthusiasm of some sponsoring organizations has waxed and waned, but the original rationale has been modified only slightly.

Throughout the program's history, the Congress, the Fellows, and the sponsoring societies have all reaped tangible benefits. To the extent that the Fellows improved the level of technical expertise on congressional staffs, thereby contributing to better legislative and public policy decisions, society as a whole has benefited, too, although perhaps in a more intangible manner.[1]

An unexpected beneficiary of the fellowship program has been the science policy community. On a theoretical level, the program has generated more material for science policy academics to analyze. On a practical level, the program has served as an avenue for bringing in new science policy practitioners. Asked to reflect upon the program's impact on channeling or launching new careers in science and technology policy, Albert Teich of the American Association for the Advancement of Science points out that some policy analysts worry that by providing an alternative path into science and technology policy, the program could diminish the importance of formal training in this area.[2]

The science and engineering fellowship program helped expand the disciplinary diversity of legislative staffs not only through the Fellows' temporary presence but also through the Fellows who remained with Congress, and by raising the awareness among congressional members that scientists and engineers can assist their work in meaningful ways.

The fellowship program also had lasting impacts outside Congress, as it helped to build a sizable cadre of politically alert scientists and engineers in key positions elsewhere in society. A cumulative impact of the program is thus the creation of a subculture of people adept at dealing with technical and political issues.

Thanks, perhaps, to these positive aspects, rationales put forth in the early 1970s remain equally viable more than 20 years later. The breadth of science- and technology-related legislative issues has expanded, reflecting problems and opportunities of modern American life. Energy and the environment, economic competitiveness, sustainable development, health care, and debates about big-ticket federal projects are all issues lending themselves to analysis by technically trained people. And while Congress employs more scientists and engineers on its permanent staff in 1994 than it did in 1974, their numbers still fall far short of the need at hand, and the Fellows program helps fill this gap.[3] The scientific and engineering communities, too, remain ever in need of renewing and expanding their firsthand knowledge of the legislative process, as new generations of practitioners (many of whom received very focused graduate educations) join the ranks.

As one long-time observer, John Andelin, has noted, we must be careful, however, not to paint "too rosy a picture" of the Congressional Science and Engineering Fellowship Program. He recalls talking to Fellows "who were at sea most of the year in Congress, and were glad to get out" and a few members who were not happy with the Fellow they had hosted. Moreover, "some Fellows became *very* political and showed little of their supposed scientific objectivity."[4] Yet Andelin maintains that the end result is unquestionably positive, for "there's no way that putting 500 of our best and brightest in Congress for a year or more wasn't immensely beneficial to the nation."[5]

One of the real, but often overlooked, accomplishments of the fellowship program is its role in stimulating and facilitating cooperation among the various scientific and engineering societies. When the fellowship programs were launched in the early 1970s, very few cooperative, cross-cutting enterprises extended beyond two professional societies. The organizational tendencies were for each group to move forward independently of the others. The very architecture of the Congressional Science and Engineering Fellowship

Conclusion

Program bridges these gaps and links seemingly disparate groups of professionals—which range from physicists and chemists to electrical and mechanical engineers, and from biologists and mathematicians to social and behavioral scientists—in a common effort.

Differences have surfaced, of course, within the coalition of societies, yet good will among their leadership—and the AAAS staff's steadfast attention to its coordinating role—has produced a lasting effort that continually sends a clear message to the legislative branch through its actions. Moreover, despite the increased emphasis on the real and perceived practical benefits of the fellowship program, the service component has never really disappeared. One of the program's greatest contributions may be, in fact, that it continues to hold forth the value of public service, reaffirming that ideal among the professions' elders and nurturing it in young scientists by example and opportunity.

APPENDIX A

Organizations Sponsoring Congressional Science and Engineering Fellows, 1973-1994

Acoustical Society of America (ASA)
    since 1977-78*
American Academy of Physician Assistants (AAPA)
    1993-94 only
American Association for Clinical Chemistry (AACC)
    1978-79 only
American Association for the Advancement of Science (AAAS)
    since 1973-74
American Association of Colleges of Pharmacy (AACP)
    since 1994-95
American Chemical Society (ACS)
    since 1975-76
American Geological Institute (AGI)
    1981-82 only
American Geophysical Union (AGU)
    since 1977-78
American Historical Association (AHA)
    1980-81 through 1985-86

*Dates of participation

APPENDIX A

American Institute of Aeronautics and Astronautics (AIAA)
   1974-75 through 1982-83
American Institute of Biological Sciences (AIBS)
   since 1984-85
American Institute of Physics (AIP)
   since 1988-89
American Mathematical Society/Mathematical Association of America/Society for Industrial and Applied Mathematics (AMS/MAA/SIAM)
   1978-79 through 1985-86
American Philosophical Association (APhA)
   1980-81 through 1985-86
American Physical Society (APS)
   since 1973-74
American Psychological Association (APA)
   since 1975-76
American Society for Horticultural Science (ASHS)
   1990-91 through 1992-93
American Society for Microbiology (ASM)
   since 1977-78
American Society for Photobiology (ASP) (with Biophysical Society)
   1981-82 through 1990-91
American Society of Agronomy/Crop Science Society of America/Soil Science Society of America/Weed Science Society of America and Regional Affiliates (ASA/CSSA/SSSA/WSSA)
   since 1989-90
American Society of Mechanical Engineers (ASME)
   since 1973-74
American Society of Plant Physiologists (ASPP)
   1989-90 through 1992-93
American Society of Zoologists (ASZ) (with American Institute of Biological Sciences)
   since 1987-88

American Veterinary Medical Association (AVMA)
    since 1988-89
Biophysical Society (BS) (with American Society for Photobiology)
    1981-82 through 1990-91
Congressional Research Service (CRS)
    1981-82 through 1982-83
Duke Roundtable on Science and Public Affairs (Duke)
    1977-78 through 1984-85
Engineering Society of Detroit (ESD)
    1981-82 through 1986-87
Federation of American Societies for Experimental Biology (FASEB)
    1975-76 through 1982-83
Federation of American Societies of Food Animal Sciences (FASFAS)
    since 1990-91
Geological Society of America (GSA)
    since 1986-87
Greater Houston Hospital Council (GHHC)
    1983-84 only
Industrial Research Institute (IRI)
    1988-89 through 1989-90
Institute of Electrical and Electronics Engineers (IEEE)
    since 1973-74
Intersociety Consortium for Plant Protection (ISCPP) (with American Institute of Biological Sciences)
    1985-86 only
National Society of Professional Engineers (NSPE)
    since 1981-82
Office of Technology Assessment (OTA)
    since 1978-79
Optical Society of America (OSA)
    1976-77 through 1979-80
Society for Research in Child Development (SRCD)
    1978-79 through 1989-90

APPENDIX A

Society for Research in Child Development (SRCD)
   1978-79 through 1989-90

Triangle Coalition for Science and Technology Education (TC)
   since 1990-91

Universities Council on Water Resources (UCOWR)
   1986-87 only

U.S. Department of Commerce Science and Technology Fellows (COMSCI)
   1985-86 only

APPENDIX B

Congressional Science and Engineering Fellows, 1973-1994

Abbotts, John (AAAS) 1985-86*
Abrahams, Edward (AHA) 1981-82
Achgill, Dennis (ASME) 1987-88
Adcock, J. Patrick (AAAS) 1988-89
Alexander, Jane (APS) 1986-87
Allen, K. Eileen (SRCD) 1981-82
Althuis, Thomas H. (ACS) 1978-79
Amaral, Deborah (ACS) 1983-84
Anderson, Elaine (APA) 1985-86
Anderson, Erma (TC) 1990-91
Anderson, Karen (APA) 1992-93
Anderson-Nielsen, Geri (TC) 1992-93
Angeli, Robert (ESD) 1983-84
Annestrand, Stig A. (IEEE) 1985-86
Aparicio, Oscar (ASM) 1993-94
Armen, Harry (ASME) 1990-91
Aroian, Lois A. (AHA) 1983-84
Atkinson, James E. (ASA) 1979-80
Aubrecht, Lyn G. (APA) 1981-82
Auchincloss, Priscilla (APS) 1990-91
Auerbach, Judith (SRCD) 1988-89
August, Diane L. (SRCD) 1983-84

*Sponsoring society and year of fellowship

Baldwin, Samuel F. (APS) 1980-81
Balmer, Norman L. (OTA) 1980-81
Balzer, Harley D. (AHA) 1982-83
Banks, R. Darryl (AAAS) 1976-77
Barbera, Robert J. (AGU) 1979-80
Barker, Robert H. (ACS) 1981-82
Barone, Charles (APA) 1993-94
Baum, Joseph (APA) 1991-92
Beall, James H. (OTA) 1978-79
Becker, Karen Marie (AVMA) 1993-94
Becker-Lausen, Evvie (APA) 1992-93
Bedesem, William B. (ASME) 1982-83
Bernabo, J. Christopher (AGU) 1978-79
Bernthal, Frederick M. (APS) 1978-79
Bierbaum, Rosina (OTA) 1980-81
Bird, Charles (MATHSOC) 1983-84
Birns, Beverly (SRCD) 1981-82
Blahous, Charles P. III (APS) 1989-90
Blockstein, David E. (AIBS/ASZ) 1987-88
Bloom-Feshbach, Jonathan (SRCD) 1980-81
Blue, Jerome H. (SRCD) 1983-84
Boardman, Barbara (OTA) 1987-88
Bohlen, Curtis C. (AIBS) 1989-90
Borthwick, Mark (Duke) 1979-80
Bostian, Charles W. (IEEE) 1988-89
Boswell, Donna (SRCD) 1985-86
Bouchard, David E. (NSPE) 1982-83
Bowser, Carl (UCOWR) 1986-87
Boyarsky, Steve (TC) 1991-92
Brecher, Aviva (APS) 1983-84
Brennan, James F. (APA) 1983-84
Brent, Bill M. (TC) 1993-94
Breton, Michael E. (OSA) 1979-80
Brown, Scott D. (SRCD) 1979-80
Bruno, Ronald C. (APS) 1976-77
Bruns, Mary Ann (OTA) 1988-89
Bryant, LeEarl Ann (IEEE) 1992-93
Bucher, David E. (COMSCI) 1985-86

Budiansky, Stephen (OTA) 1985-86
Butler, Dixon M. (APS) 1979-80
Butler, Eric L. (AGU) 1984-85
Butrimovitz, Gerald P. (AACC) 1978-79
Buyrn, Audrey B. (AAAS) 1975-76
Cahn, Jerry (SRCD) 1979-80
Caldwell, Cleopatra H. (SRCD) 1986-87
Canan, Pat (TC) 1992-93
Carmi, Shlomo (ESD) 1985-86
Carpenter, Jeffrey (ASPP) 1992-93
Carrow, Grant M. (AAAS) 1990-91
Cartier, Joan (APS) 1988-89
Cech, Irina (AAAS) 1989-90
Chafel, Judith A. (SRCD) 1989-90
Chambers, Lyn (AAAS) 1977-78
Chan, Yupo (OTA) 1979-80
Charo, Arthur (AIP) 1988-89
Chase-Lansdale, P. Lindsay (SRCD) 1981-82
Cheng, Dean (OTA) 1993-94
Chmielewski, Donna L. (AAAS/SRCD) 1978-79
Chu, John T. (MATHSOC) 1982-83
Ciric, Ljiljana (ASME) 1992-93
Claridge, David (AAAS) 1975-76
Clement, John R.B. (SRCD) 1984-85
Clough, John M., Jr. (AAAS/ASP) 1980-81
Coccio, Christopher L. (ASME) 1975-76
Colborn, Theo (OTA) 1985-86
Cole, David (APhA) 1985-86
Colglazier, E. William, Jr. (AAAS) 1976-77
Collings, Walter (AIAA) 1977-78
Cook, Lynne (SRCD) 1986-87
Cook-Deegan, Robert (OTA) 1982-83
Cooper, Benjamin S. (APS) 1973-74
Cooper, Ralph E. (APA) 1977-78
Cooper, Thomas E. (ASME) 1975-76
Copeland, Curtis (GHHC) 1983-84
Copeland, Guy L. (IEEE) 1983-84
Corbin, David A. (AHA) 1983-84

APPENDIX B

Corn, M. Lynne (AAAS/ASZ) 1979-80
Cornehls, James V. (OTA) 1978-79
Cornell, E. Kevin (AAAS) 1974-75
Corrigan, Donald (COMSCI) 1985-86
Corrigan, Jacqueline (OTA) 1990-91
Cortner, Hanna J. (UCOWR) 1986-87
Cox, James E. (ASME) 1974-75
Craig, Daniel (Duke) 1980-81
Craine, Lloyd B. (IEEE) 1974-75
Cranor, Carl (APhA) 1985-86
Crilly, Paul (IEEE) 1993-94
Crisp, Michael D. (OSA) 1976-77
Cromartie, William J. (AAAS) 1982-83
Cross-Kramer, Teresa S. (Duke) 1982-83
Crowley, Julia C. (OTA) 1982-83
Cummins, Michael (ESD) 1986-87
Curran, Linda M. (OTA) 1981-82
Curran, Nancy Morency (APA) 1979-80
Dale, Steinar J. (IEEE) 1986-87
Danello, Mary Ann T. (ASM) 1981-82
D'Annucci, Robert R. (Duke) 1979-80
Davis, Miriam (CRS) 1982-83
DeGraw, Christopher (SRCD) 1988-89
Delp, Charles (AIBS/ISCPP) 1985-86
Denison, Richard A. (OTA) 1984-85
Denney, James (ASHS) 1992-93
Dickey, Joseph W. (ASA) 1983-84
Dickson, Mark Kevin (ACS) 1984-85
Diehn, Bodo (ACS) 1975-76
Dierauf, Leslie (AVMA) 1990-91
Dillon, Robert T., Jr. (OTA) 1981-82
Dobert, Raymond (ASPP) 1990-91
Donnelly, Anne H. Cohn (SRCD) 1978-79
Donnelly, Patrick (FASFAS) 1991-92
Doty, Pamela (OTA) 1979-80
Drehoff, Diane W. (IEEE) 1975-76
Dundon, Stanislaus J. (APhA) 1980-81
Dunivin, Debra Lina (AAAS/APA) 1992-94

Eck, David (ACS) 1979-80
Edminister, Joseph A. (IEEE) 1983-84
Edwards, Carol E. (OTA) 1991-92
Elam, Tim (AIP) 1990-91
Elfring, Chris (OTA) 1979-80
Ellis, Gary B. (OTA) 1983-84
Ellson, Robert (ASME) 1990-91
Engquist-Seidenberg, Gretchen (Duke) 1978-79
Epstein, Gerald L. (OTA) 1983-84
Evans, James E. (GSA) 1987-88
Everett, Barbara A. (SRCD) 1979-80
Eyring, Greg (OTA) 1984-85
Faas, Richard W. (AGI) 1981-82
Fagan, Thomas L. (IEEE) 1979-80
Fainberg, Anthony (APS) 1983-84
Farber, David (AHA) 1985-86
Fathe, Laurie (APS) 1992-93
Faulkner, Lloyd C. (FASEB) 1976-77
Feldman, Diane T. (Duke) 1981-82
Fellows, Jack D. (AGU) 1983-84
Fenstermacher, Dan L. (AAAS) 1991-92
Fernandez, Michael (ASPP) 1991-92
Finck, Joseph (APS) 1985-86
Finnegan, Niall (AVMA) 1992-93
Fischer, Eric (AAAS) 1987-88
Flattau, Pamela Ebert (AAAS/APA) 1974-75
Foster, William (SRCD) 1987-88
Fox, Barbara (SRCD) 1987-88
Frank, Barbara (AGU) 1989-90
Franklin, Earl (ASME) 1981-82
Freire, Maria C. (BS/ASP) 1984-86
Friedman, Louis D. (AIAA) 1978-79
Friedman, Robert M. (OTA) 1978-79
Frizzell, Virgil A., Jr. (AGU) 1988-89
Frohboese, Robinsue (APA) 1980-81
Froman, Lawrence (APA) 1975-76
Fromm, Eli (IEEE) 1980-81
Fruci, Jean (ASA/AIBS) 1993-94

Furtek, Edward C. (Duke) 1977-78
Gallin, Elaine K. (BS) 1988-89
Garant, Raymond (ACS) 1992-93
Gardner, Charles (ASM) 1991-92
Gardner, Kenneth D., Jr. (FASEB) 1979-80
Garduque, Laurie (SRCD) 1983-84
Garin, David L. (ACS) 1980-81
Garrison, Ellen Greenberg (SRCD) 1982-83
Garwood, S. Gray (SRCD) 1982-83
Gasque, Betty (TC) 1991-92
Gaster, Robin (OTA) 1989-90
Gearhart, Martha S. (AVMA) 1988-89
Geer, Kristen A. (AAAS) 1988-89
Gibbons, Lillian K. (SRCD) 1980-81
Gillroy, John M. (APhA) 1985-86
Gilman, J. Paul (AAAS) 1978-79
Glowinski, Irene (ACS) 1985-86
Gluck, Michael E. (OTA) 1987-88
Gnam, Rosemarie (AIBS/ASZ) 1991-92
Goettel, Kenneth (AIP) 1989-90
Goldin, Edwin (APS) 1987-88
Goodman, Mark (AIP) 1992-93
Goud Collins, Margaret (GSA) 1992-93
Gover, James E. (IEEE) 1987-88
Grady, Judith R. (ESD) 1983-84
Grayson, Lawrence P. (IEEE) 1986-87
Greene, James C. (ACS) 1980-81
Greger, Janet L. (AAAS) 1984-85
Griffith, Gwendolyn (AVMA) 1991-92
Grulke, Eric A. (ESD) 1981-82
Gunn, Elizabeth (OTA) 1993-94
Hafemeister, David W. (AAAS) 1975-76
Haimes, Yacov Y. (AGU) 1977-78
Hall, Blair (COMSCI) 1985-86
Hammer, Philip (APS) 1993-94
Handelsman, Mitchell M. (APA) 1989-90
Hanlon, Daniel E. (ESD) 1985-86
Hannah, Lee (AIBS) 1986-87

Harclerode, Howard C. II (NSPE) 1981-82
Hare, John E. (APhA) 1981-82
Harper, Jerome P. (AAAS) 1974-75
Harrison, Helen (ASHS) 1991-92
Hartman, Andrew J. (SRCD) 1983-84
Haskins, Ron (SRCD) 1985-86
Hatziandreu, Evridiki (OTA) 1989-90
Heidbreder, Glenn R. (IEEE) 1981-82
Heller, Miriam (OTA) 1983-84
Henderson, Tracey (ASA/AIBS) 1993-94
Hersh, Richard H. (OTA) 1982-83
Hess, J. Richard (ASA/CSSA/SSSA/WSSA) 1992-93
Hess, Jennifer (GSA) 1986-87
Hitzman, Murray W. (GSA) 1993-94
Hodges, Carroll Ann (AGU) 1980-81
Hoffman, Allan R. (APS) 1974-75
Holliday, Bertha G. (SRCD) 1985-86
Holt, Rush D. (APS) 1982-83
Holte, Kirby C. (IEEE) 1976-77
Horrigan, Sarah (ASM) 1990-91
Horwitz, Paul (APS) 1975-76
Howes, Ruth (AAAS) 1993-94
Hudson, Kathy Lynn (ASM) 1989-90/(OTA) 1990-91
Hughes, Lucian (OTA) 1992-93
Huntington, Gail S. (SRCD) 1989-90
Hurley, Frank (AIAA) 1976-77
Hurwicz, Henryk (ASME) 1991-92
Huyck, Heather (AHA) 1985-86
Hyman, Barry I. (ASME) 1973-74
Hyman, Eric L. (OTA) 1982-83
Imgram, Donald A. (AIAA) 1981-82
Indrisano, Victor (APA) 1984-85
Isherwood, Dana (AGU) 1985-86
Ives, Catherine Lynn (ASM) 1992-93
Izzo, Ralph (APS) 1984-85
Jackson, Anthony Wells (SRCD) 1982-83
Jacobson, George L., Jr. (AAAS) 1976-77
Jaeger, Richard J. (IEEE) 1991-92

APPENDIX B

James, Ann N. (ASM) 1979-80
Joellenbeck, Lois (OTA) 1993-94
Johnson, Clark E. (IEEE) 1987-88
Johnson, David H. (Duke) 1981-82
Johnson, David W. (ASA/CSSA/SSSA/WSSA) 1990-91
Johnson, Ernest W. (AAAS) 1975-76
Kaarsberg, Tina (APS) 1991-92
Kagan, Constance H. (APhA) 1981-82
Kainz, Robert J. (CRS) 1982-83
Katz, Sidney (FASEB) 1980-81
Kaufman, Don A. (ACS) 1983-84
Keblawi, Feisal S. (IEEE) 1981-82
Keel, Alton G., Jr. (AIAA) 1977-78
Kelly, Henry C. (AAAS) 1974-75
Kennedy, May (APA) 1988-89
Kennedy, Robert (ASME) 1993-94
King, Andrea B. (APhA) 1984-85
King, Denis J. (IEEE) 1988-89
Kirkpatrick, Wallace E. (AIAA) 1979-80
Kleineberg, Gerd A. (OTA) 1980-81
Koch, Susan (OTA) 1986-87
Kohrman, Arthur F. (OTA) 1980-81
Komor, Paul S. (OTA) 1989-90
Koppatschek, Fritz K. (ASA/CSSA/SSSA/WSSA) 1989-90
Korbin, Jill (SRCD) 1985-86
Koretz, Daniel M. (APA) 1978-79
Kovacs, Karen (APA) 1993-94
Kram, Malcolm A. (AVMA) 1989-90
Krasnow, Richard (AAAS) 1981-82
Kreid, Dennis K. (ASME) 1980-81
Kunkel, Dale L. (SRCD) 1984-85
Kuznetsov, Stephen B. (NSPE) 1983-84
Ladd, Theodore B. (COMSCI) 1985-86
LaFollette, Marcel C. (OTA) 1984-85
Landolt, Robert G. (ACS) 1986-87
Lang, Valerie (AGU) 1992-93
Larsen, Lawrence E. (IEEE) 1992-93
Larson, Ronal (IEEE) 1973-74

Lau, K.P. (IEEE) 1984-85
Leber, R. Eric (AAAS) 1977-78
Lebofsky, Arthur (TC) 1990-91
Lee, E. Gregory (MATHSOC) 1978-79
Lee, Eileen (ASM) 1985-86
Lee, JoAnn (APA) 1990-91
Lefkoff, Jeff (AGU) 1986-87
Legendre, Philip J. (ASME) 1981-82
Leitch, Bonnie (TC) 1993-94
Lengnick, Laura (ASA/CSSA) 1991-92
Lenz, Ernest (AAAS/APA) 1992-93
Leshowitz, Barry H. (ASA) 1977-78
Levenson, Howard (OTA) 1983-84
Levine, Marc V. (AHA) 1983-84
Lewis, Catherine C. (Duke) 1980-81
Lewis, David C. (IEEE) 1978-79
Lin, Herbert (AAAS) 1986-87
Lo, Thomas (ASME) 1979-80
Londono, Carmina (AIP) 1993-94
Long, Edward R. (AHA) 1982-83
Lubin, Barry T. (ASME) 1979-80
Lubowsky, Jack (IEEE) 1982-83
Maclin, Arlene (OTA) 1978-79
Maga, Timothy P. (AHA) 1984-85
Mann, Curt J. (AVMA) 1991-92
Marin, Philip (ASME) 1977-78
Martin, Jerry L. (APHA) 1982-83
Martin, John F. (Duke) 1977-78
Marvel, Orin E. (IEEE) 1982-83
Mastracco, James M. (ASA) 1989-90
Mathews, Jessica Tuchman (AAAS) 1973-74
Matos, Frederick (IEEE) 1986-87
Maxwell, Paul C. (APS) 1977-78
Mayer, John A., Jr. (ASME) 1976-77
McCaughan, Della (TC) 1991-92
McGinty, Kathleen Alana (ACS) 1989-90
McNutt, Kristen W. (FASEB) 1977-78
Meezan, William A. (SRCD) 1984-85

Appendix B

Meyers, Judith C. (APA) 1982-83
Milford, Jana (OTA) 1987-88
Mitchell, Edna M. (SRCD) 1980-81
Moomaw, William R. (AAAS) 1975-76
Moore, Duncan T. (APS) 1993-94
Morse, Gale (OTA) 1988-89
Moss, Thomas H. (APS) 1974-75
Muller, Burton H. (APS) 1980-81
Murphy, James R. (MATHSOC) 1985-86
Myers, Robert L. (ASA) 1988-89
Myers-Bohlke, Brenda (NSPE) 1987-88
Nelson, Burke E. (ASME) 1974-75
Nelson, Miriam E. (AAAS) 1987-88
Newell, Nanette (OTA) 1981-82
Nishimi, Robyn Y. (ASM) 1983-84
Nissim-Sabat, Denis (APA) 1989-90
Noonan, Norine E. (ACS) 1982-83
Norberg, Ann Marie (ASM) 1978-79
Nordal, Katherine (APA) 1990-91
Nusbaum, Kenneth E. (AVMA) 1992-93
Oaks, Sherry D. (AGU) 1987-88
Oberg, Charles N. (SRCD) 1984-85
Olson, Patricia (AVMA) 1993-94
Pachter, Wendy (APA) 1988-89
Palmer, Robert (AAAS) 1979-80
Pan, Vivian (AGU) 1991-92
Panshin, Daniel A. (OTA) 1978-79
Parker, Sydney Ruth (Duke) 1977-78
Parvin, Ruth Ann (APA) 1985-86
Paterno, Philip M. (IEEE) 1989-90
Pautler, Eugene L. (FASEB) 1981-82
Payne, Jeffrey (AGU) 1990-91
Pearlman, Althea (TC) 1991-92
Pearson, Willie, Jr. (OTA) 1988-89
Peery, J. Craig (SRCD) 1980-81
Perry, Clifton (APhA) 1983-84
Pestak, Mark W. (APS) 1988-89
Pestorius, Thomas D. (ASME) 1980-81

Pharis, Mary (SRCD) 1979-80
Philips, William (TC) 1990-91
Phillips, Deborah A. (SRCD) 1981-82
Pizzigati, Karabelle (SRCD) 1978-79
Polan, Susan (AAAS) 1992-93
Polenicek, John G. (AAPA) 1993-94
Pollard, William J. (ESD) 1982-83
Pomerantz, David (APhA) 1982-83
Porter, Donna V. (AAAS) 1980-81
Portmess, Lisa (APhA) 1985-86
Prabhakar, Arati (OTA) 1984-85
Preston, Ron (Duke) 1978-79
Puglisi, J. Thomas (APA) 1986-87
Puka, William (APhA) 1980-81
Pullen, John Mark (IEEE) 1985-86
Quraishi, Rana (AIBS) 1984-85
Rahn, Ronald O. (ASP/BS) 1983-84
Ramonas, Lori M. (ACS) 1981-82
Randal, Judith (OTA) 1980-81
Rauch-Elnekave, Helen (SRCD) 1981-82
Recker, David (OTA) 1990-91
Reese, David K. (ASME) 1988-89
Reichert, Joshua S. (Duke) 1980-81
Reinhard, David William (AHA) 1981-82
Rickel, Annette U. (AAAS/APA) 1992-93
Riebling, Robert W. (AIAA) 1980-81
Rigas, Anthony L. (IEEE) 1975-76
Ritchie, Gary A. (AAAS) 1976-77
Ritts, Rosalyn (AIP) 1991-92
Robinson, Elizabeth (GSA) 1988-89
Robock, Alan (AAAS) 1986-87
Roca, Richard T. (ASME) 1976-77
Romm, Joseph (APS) 1987-88
Rosenbaum, Harold (AIAA) 1975-76
Rosenberg, Allison A. (APA) 1991-92
Rosenberg, Zeda F. (ASM) 1982-83
Rosenheck, Albert (IEEE) 1993-94
Ross, Melvin (ASME) 1985-86

Appendix B

Roy, Robin (OTA) 1987-88
Rubin, Michael B. (ASME) 1989-90
Russell, Lesley M. (ASM) 1984-85
Ryan, James (OTA) 1980-81
Saiki, Margaret (AVMA) 1992-93
Sarewitz, Daniel R. (GSA) 1989-90
Saterson, Kathryn A. (AIBS) 1985-86
Satterfield, Doyce E. (IEEE) 1982-83
Saundry, Peter (APS) 1991-92
Saxe, Leonard (OTA) 1978-79
Scanlon, William J. (OTA) 1978-79
Schaefer, Mark (OTA) 1987-88
Schatte, Christopher L. (FASEB) 1978-79
Schiffries, Craig M. (GSA) 1990-91
Schiller, Carol (ACS) 1985-86
Schmid, Charles (ASA) 1985-86
Schurr, Sara C. (APA) 1976-77
Schwartz, Rosalie (AHA) 1980-81
Scotch, Richard K. (SRCD) 1982-83
Searle, Maureen (Duke) 1983-84
Segal, Elizabeth (SRCD) 1988-89
Segal, Elliot A. (AAAS) 1973-74
Segar, Douglas A. (OSA) 1977-78
Shapira, Philip (OTA) 1986-87
Sharma, Dharmendra K. (IEEE) 1990-91
Sharples, Frances E. (AAAS) 1984-85
Shaw, George H. (AGU) 1981-82
Sheahen, Thomas P. (APS) 1977-78
Shearer, Clement F. (AAAS) 1977-78
Siegel, Jay A. (ACS) 1988-89
Siemens, Angela (FASFAS) 1990-91
Sierra, Ricardo (NSPE) 1993-94
Silber, Bohne G. (APA) 1984-85
Silverstein, Arthur M. (FASEB) 1975-76
Simmons, James (Duke) 1979-80
Simpson, Michael M. (CRS) 1981-82
Simpson, Theodore R. (IEEE) 1980-81
Singleton, Rivers, Jr. (ASM) 1988-89

Smedley, Brian (APA) 1993-94
Smith, Gordon A. (AIAA) 1982-83
Smith, Granville (APS) 1976-77
Smith, P. Gene (IEEE) 1979-80
Smith, Robert Burleson (ASA/WSSA) 1991-92
Smith, Sheila (SRCD) 1986-87
Smith, Willis D. (IEEE) 1974-75
Smythe, Robert T. (MATHSOC) 1979-80
Snowdon, Jill A. (ASM) 1987-88
Sokkappa, Balraj G. (IEEE) 1977-78
Sokolove, Phillip (FASEB) 1982-83
Solarz, Andrea L. (APA) 1987-88
Solovey, Garrick J. (ASME) 1982-83
Sponsler, George Curtis III (IEEE) 1987-88
St. Hilaire, Cathy Reed (ASM) 1977-78
Staiger, Roger P., Jr. (ASME) 1978-79
Stanton, Marsha A. (ASA/CSSA/SSSA/WSSA) 1992-93
Starr, Raymond H. (SRCD) 1980-81
Statuto, Carol M. (SRCD) 1982-83
Stein, Donald G. (AAAS) 1980-81
Stern, Larry (IEEE) 1991-92
Stevens, T. Christine (MATHSOC) 1984-85
Stewart, Krista J. (APA) 1987-88
Stine, Jeffrey K. (AHA) 1984-85
Stipek, Deborah J. (SRCD) 1983-84
Stoll, Ulrich W. (ESD) 1981-82
Stonner, David M. (APA) 1982-83
Strauss, Harlee (BS/ASP) 1981-82
Strickler, Robert L. (AIAA) 1979-80
Sutton, Michael (ACS) 1987-88
Sweedler, Alan R. (APS) 1984-85
Swetnam, George F. (IEEE) 1983-84
Szopo, Irene E. (OTA) 1978-79
Takanishi, Ruby (SRCD) 1980-81
Tananbaum, Duane A. (AHA) 1980-81
Tao, Winston (AGU) 1993-94
Taylor, Kenneth B. (GSA) 1991-92
Taylor, Kerry (AVMA) 1993-94

Taylor, Melanie-Anne (APA) 1991-92
Telson, Michael L. (AAAS) 1973-74
Tennant, Mark H. (ASME) 1982-83
Theiss, Susan (OTA) 1981-82
Thomas, Gary L. (AAAS) 1974-75
Thomas, Nancy G. (SRCD) 1987-88
Treglio, James R. (APS) 1982-83
Tropf, Cheryl G. (MATHSOC) 1980-81
Tumeo, Mark A. (AAAS) 1993-94
Tunis, Sean (AAAS) 1991-92
Twogood, Frederick J. (IEEE) 1980-81
Tyszkiewicz, Mary (ACS) 1993-94
Uebelhoer, Jane F. (APhA) 1983-84
Valleroy, Linda (AAAS) 1986-87
Vanderpool, Janet E. (ESD) 1984-85
van der Vink, Gregory (OTA) 1985-86
Veigel, Jon M. (AAAS) 1974-75
Vereen, Alonzo (ESD) 1984-85
Victor, Alfred E. (IEEE) 1989-90
Vincent, Trudy (APA) 1986-87
Vischi, Thomas (OTA) 1992-93
Waggoner, Charlene M. (ASPP) 1989-90
Wagner, Kathryn D. (OTA) 1985-86
Wagner, Kenneth D. (IEEE) 1991-92
Wagner, Marta (AHA) 1984-85
Wagner, Scott M. (ESD) 1982-83
Wallace, John B. (IEEE) 1977-78
Walsh, Marie E. (OTA) 1988-89
Ware, Randolph (OTA) 1983-84
Washington, Valora (SRCD) 1981-82
Watkins, Bruce A. (SRCD) 1984-85
Weatherford, Jack McIver (SRCD) 1978-79
Wedding, Danny (APA) 1990-91
Wedin, Randall E. (ACS) 1982-83
Weiner, Elliot (APA) 1993-94
Weiner, Ruth F. (AAAS) 1983-84
Weis, Judith S. (AAAS/ASZ) 1983-84
Weiss, Leonard (IEEE) 1975-76

Weisse, Herb (NSPE) 1986-87
Weissman, Arthur B. (AGU) 1982-83
Wentworth, Diane K. (Duke) 1983-84
Werthamer, N. Richard (APS) 1973-74
Westendorf, Michael L. (FASFAS) 1992-93
White, Karl R. (SRCD) 1984-85
Whiteside, Haven (APS) 1974-75
Whitman, Carol (ASA/CSSA/SSSA) 1990-91
Whyte, Ian A. (IEEE) 1978-79
Widnall, William S. (AIAA) 1974-75
Wilcox, Brian L. (SRCD) 1984-85
Williams, Henry N. (ASM) 1980-81
Williamson, Ray A. (OTA) 1979-80
Willyard, Donald L. (IEEE) 1990-91
Wilson, Ann L. (SRCD) 1982-83
Wilson, L. George (ASHS) 1990-91
Wilt, J. Christopher (NSPE) 1985-86
Wittels, Jill J. (APS) 1978-79
Witwer, Jeffrey (ASME) 1977-78
Woldin, Richard (ASME) 1978-79
Wolf, Charlie P. (AAAS) 1975-76
Wood, Susan (BS) 1990-91
Woods, Robert (ASME) 1991-92
Yamashita, June J.M. (TC) 1990-91
Young, John H. (APS) 1975-76
Yudken, Joel (AAAS) 1992-93
Zeiger, Alice V. (ACS) 1986-87
Ziehe, Gary (FASFAS) 1993-94
Ziman, Stephen D. (ACS) 1979-80
Zimmerman, Marc A. (OTA) 1988-89
Zot, Anita (AAAS) 1990-91
Zucker, Deborah (ASM) 1986-87
Zuckerman, Diana M. (APA) 1983-84

APPENDIX C

Congressional Offices and Committees Participating in the Science and Engineering Fellowship Program, 1973-1994

Offices of Current Senators

Senator Max S. Baucus
Senator Jeff Bingaman
Senator Barbara Boxer
Senator Bill Bradley
Senator Dale Bumpers
Senator Thad Cochran
Senator Kent Conrad
Senator Alfonse M. D'Amato
Senator Thomas A. Daschle
Senator Christopher J. Dodd
Senator Robert Dole
Senator Pete V. Domenici
Senator David F. Durenberger
Senator Wendell H. Ford
Senator John Glenn
Senator Slade Gorton

APPENDIX C

Senator Tom Harkin
Senator Mark O. Hatfield
Senator Howell T. Heflin
Senator Daniel K. Inouye
Senator Edward M. Kennedy
Senator J. Robert Kerrey
Senator Frank R. Lautenberg
Senator Patrick J. Leahy
Senator Carl Levin
Senator Barbara A. Mikulski
Senator Bob Packwood
Senator Harry Reid
Senator Donald W. Riegle, Jr.
Senator John D. Rockefeller IV
Senator William V. Roth, Jr.
Senator Paul Simon
Senator Alan K. Simpson
Senator Arlen Specter
Senator Ted Stevens
Senator Strom Thurmond
Senator John W. Warner
Senator Paul David Wellstone

Offices of Former Senators

Senator Howard Baker
Senator Alan Cranston
Senator Jeremiah Denton
Senator Albert Gore, Jr.
Senator Gary K. Hart
Senator Philip Hart
Senator Paula Hawkins
Senator Warren Magnuson
Senator Charles Mathias
Senator William Proxmire
Senator Dan Quayle
Senator Terry Sanford

Senator Harrison Schmitt
Senator Paul Tsongas
Senator Timothy E. Wirth

Offices of Current Representatives

Representative Michael A. Andrews
Representative Jim Bacchus
Representative George E. Brown, Jr.
Representative Anna G. Eshoo
Representative Vic Fazio
Representative Richard A. Gephardt
Representative Pete Geren
Representative Lee H. Hamilton
Representative Tom Lantos
Representative Sander M. Levin
Representative Edward J. Markey
Representative Joseph M. McDade
Representative George Miller
Representative Norman Y. Mineta
Representative Patsy T. Mink
Representative Austin J. Murphy
Representative David R. Obey
Representative Charles B. Rangel
Representative J. Roy Rowland
Representative Rick Santorum
Representative Steven H. Schiff
Representative Patricia Schroeder
Representative Philip R. Sharp
Representative Louise M. Slaughter
Representative Charles W. Stenholm
Representative Al Swift
Representative Jolene Unsoeld
Representative Pat Williams

APPENDIX C

Offices of Former Representatives

Representative Charles E. Bennett
Representative Mario Biaggi
Representative Don Bonker
Representative William Broadhead
Representative Hank Brown
Representative Byron L. Dorgan
Representative Robert Drinan
Representative Mervyn M. Dymally
Representative Roy Dyson
Representative Dennis E. Eckart
Representative Robert W. Edgar
Representative Allen E. Ertle
Representative Mike Espy
Representative Don Fuqua
Representative Albert Gore, Jr.
Representative Bill Green
Representative Judd Gregg
Representative Cecil Heftel
Representative James M. Jeffords
Representative Jack F. Kemp
Representative Robert L. Legget
Representative Clarence Long
Representative Andrew Maguire
Representative Michael McCormack
Representative Howard M. Metzenbaum
Representative Barbara A. Mikulski
Representative Abner J. Mikva
Representative Bruce A. Morrison
Representative Charles Mosher
Representative Don Ritter
Representative Edward R. Roybal
Representative James Santini
Representative Claudine Schneider
Representative Paul Simon
Representative Stephen J. Solarz

PARTICIPATING OFFICES

Representative Mac Sweeney
Representative Thomas J. Tauke
Representative Morris K. Udall
Representative Doug Walgren
Representative Ted Weiss
Representative Howard Wolpe
Representative James C. Wright
Representative Ed Zschau

Congressional Committees and Subcommittees

Senate Committee on Aerospace*
Senate Committee on Agriculture*
Senate Committee on Agriculture, Nutrition, and Forestry
Senate Committee on Armed Services
Senate Committee on the Budget
Senate Committee on Commerce, Science, and Transportation
Senate Committee on Energy and Natural Resources
Senate Committee on Environment and Public Works
Senate Committee on Finance
Senate Committee on Foreign Relations
Senate Committee on Governmental Affairs
Senate Committee on the Interior*
Senate Committee on the Interior and Insular Affairs*
Senate Committee on Labor and Human Resources
Senate Select Committee on Intelligence

Senate Subcommittee on Aging (Labor and Human Resources)
Senate Subcommittee on Children and Youth (Labor and Human Resources)*
Senate Subcommittee on Children, Family, Drugs and Alcoholism (Labor and Human Resources)
Senate Subcommittee on Disabilities (Labor and Human Resources)*

Former or renamed committees and subcommittees

Appendix C

Senate Subcommittee on Education, Arts, and Humanities (Labor and Human Resources)
Senate Subcommittee on Energy, Nuclear Proliferation, and Government Affairs (Energy and Natural Resources)*
Senate Subcommittee on Energy Research and Development (Energy and Natural Resources)
Senate Subcommittee on Health (Finance)*
Senate Subcommittee on Health (Labor and Public Welfare)*
Senate Subcommittee on Health and Human Services (Appropriations)*
Senate Subcommittee on Housing and Urban Affairs (Banking, Housing, and Urban Affairs)
Senate Subcommittee on Human Resources and Intergovernmental Relations (Government Operations)*
Senate Subcommittee on Juvenile Justice (Judiciary)
Senate Subcommittee on Labor, Health and Human Services, Education, and Related Agencies (Appropriations)
Senate Subcommittee on Science, Technology, and Space (Commerce, Science, and Transportation)
Senate Subcommittee on Technology and the Law (Judiciary)
Senate Subcommittee on Toxic Substances and Environmental Oversight (Environment and Public Works)*
Senate Subcommittee on Veterans Affairs, Housing and Urban Development, and Independent Agencies (Appropriations)

House Committee on Agriculture
House Committee on Armed Services
House Committee on Banking, Finance, and Urban Affairs
House Committee on Education*
House Committee on Energy and Commerce
House Committee on Government Operations

* *Former or renamed committees and subcommittees*

PARTICIPATING OFFICES

House Committee on Interior and Insular Affairs*
House Committee on Interstate and Foreign Commerce*
House Committee on Merchant Marine and Fisheries
House Committee on Science, Space, and Technology
House Committee on Ways and Means
House Select Committee on Aging*
House Select Committee on Children, Youth, and Families*
House Select Committee on Hunger*

House Subcommittee on Asia and the Pacific (Foreign Affairs)
House Subcommittee on Child and Human Development (Labor and Human Resources)*
House Subcommittee on Commerce, Transportation, and Tourism (Energy and Commerce)*
House Subcommittee on Department Operations, Research, and Foreign Agriculture (Agriculture)*
House Subcommittee on Elementary, Secondary, and Vocational Education (Education and Labor)
House Subcommittee on Energy and Power (Energy and Commerce)
House Subcommittee on Energy, Conservation, and Power (Energy and Commerce)*
House Subcommittee on Energy Development and Applications (Science and Technology)*
House Subcommittee on Energy Research and Development (Science and Technology)*
House Subcommittee on the Environment (Science, Space, and Technology)*
House Subcommittee on Environment, Energy, and Natural Resources (Government Operations)
House Subcommittee on General Oversight and Investigations (Energy and Commerce)*
House Subcommittee on Human Resources and Intergovernmental Relations (Government Operations)
House Subcommittee on International Cooperation in Science (Science, Space, and Technology)*

* *Former or renamed committees and subcommittees*

APPENDIX C

House Subcommittee on International Development, Institutions, and Finance (Banking, Finance, and Urban Affairs)*
House Subcommittee on Investigations and Oversight (Science, Space, and Technology)
House Subcommittee on Livestock, Dairy, and Poultry (Agriculture)*
House Subcommittee on National Parks and Recreation (Interior)*
House Subcommittee on National Parks, Forests, and Public Lands (Natural Resources)
House Subcommittee on Natural Resources, Agricultural Research, and Environment (Science, Space, and Technology)*
House Subcommittee on Oversight and Investigations (Energy and Commerce)
House Subcommittee on Public Lands, National Parks, and Forests (Natural Resources)*
House Subcommittee on Science (Science, Space, and Technology)
House Subcommittee on Science, Research, and Technology (Science and Technology)*
House Subcommittee on Space Science and Applications (Science, Space, and Technology)*
House Subcommittee on Technology and Competitiveness (Science, Space, and Technology)*
House Subcommittee on Telecommunications and Finance (Energy and Commerce)
House Subcommittee on Transportation, Aviation, and Materials (Science, Space, and Technology)*

Other Congressional Offices

Congressional Budget Office
Congressional Caucus for Women's Issues
Congressional Research Service
Office of Technology Assessment
Senate Democratic Policy Committee
* *Former or renamed committees and subcommittees*

APPENDIX D

Directors of the Congressional Science and Engineering Fellowship Program, 1973-1994

Richard A. Scribner	1973-1978
Charles Mosher	1978-1979
William G. Wells, Jr.	1979-1980
Richard A. Scribner	1980-1984
Stephen D. Nelson	1984-present

ENDNOTES

Foreword

1. This foreword draws from the following materials, which are available in the Claudia Sturges Congressional Fellows collection, AAAS Archives, Washington, D.C., except as otherwise noted: William T. Golden to Joel R. Primack, 5 April 1972 [regarding Robert Oppenheimer and Charles Lauritsen]; William T. Golden to William Drayton, 10 January 1973; memorandum, William Drayton to Former Fellow AAAS Youth Council Members, 22 January 1973; William Drayton to Joel R. Primack, 21 February 1973; William T. Golden to Joel R. Primack, 14 March 1980; William T. Golden to Michael Telson and Albert Teich, 12 August 1987; memorandum, William T. Golden to Albert Teich and Michael Telson, 12 August 1987 [regarding initial funding]; talks by William T. Golden and Michael L. Telson at the 20th Anniversary Celebration of the AAAS Congressional Science and Engineering Fellows, Washington, D.C., 30 September 1993; "Inside AAAS: 20th Anniversary of Congressional Fellowship Program," *Science*, 261 (August 27, 1993), 1190-1191; Carnegie Commission on Science, Technology, and Government, *Science, Technology, and Congress: Expert Advice and the Decision-Making Process* (New York: Carnegie Commission on Science, Technology, and Government, February 1991) [recommends strengthening and expansion of the Congressional Science and Engineering Fellowship Program]; and William T. Golden, "Government Military-Scientific Research: Review for the President of the United States, 1950-51," basic documents, including precept, report, memoranda, and interviews with about 150 appropriate individuals (unpublished manuscript, 432 pages: copies available at the Harry S. Truman Library, Independence, MO; the library of the American Institute of Physics, College Park, MD; the Herbert Hoover Library, West Branch, IA; the Dwight D. Eisenhower Library, Abilene, KS; and the Library of Congress, Washington, D.C.).

Preface

1. Several articles highlight the contributions of the science and engineering Fellows, including: Richard A. Scribner and Mary L. Shoaf, "Four Years of Congressional Science Fellows," *Physics Today*, 30 (August 1977), 36-40; Barry M. Casper, "Scientists on the Hill," *Bulletin of the Atomic Scientists*, 33 (November 1977), 8-15; Richard A. Scribner, "Congressional Science Fellows: A Bridge to Better Understanding and Public Policy," *Grants Magazine*, 1 (September 1978), 206-217; and Michael L. Telson and Albert H. Teich, "Science Advice to the Congress: The Congressional Science and Engineering Fellows Program," in William T. Golden (ed.), *Science and Technology Advice to the President, Congress, and Judiciary* (New York: Pergamon Press, 1988 [second edition; Washington: AAAS Press, 1993]), pp. 447-453.

Chapter 1

1. These developments are discussed in Jeffrey K. Stine, *A History of Science Policy in the United States, 1940-1985*, Background Report No. 1, Task Force on Science Policy, House Committee on Science and Technology, 99th Cong., 2nd sess. (Washington: GPO, 1986); and Bruce L. R. Smith, *American Science Policy since World War II* (Washington: The Brookings Institution, 1990). For the impact of these trends on academic science and engineering, see Roger L. Geiger, *Research and Relevant Knowledge: American Research Universities since World War II* (New York: Oxford University Press, 1993). For the evolution of public attitudes toward scientists and engineers, see Marcel C. LaFollette, *Making Science Our Own: Public Images of Science, 1910-1955* (Chicago: The University of Chicago Press, 1990).

2. See Stine, *A History of Science Policy in the United States*, pp. 57-70; Geiger, *Research and Relevant Knowledge*, pp. 230-269; and Stuart W. Leslie, *The Cold War and American Science: The Military-Industrial-Academic Complex at MIT and Stanford* (New York: Columbia University Press, 1993), pp. 233-256. For an overview of the political and cultural tenor of the 1970s, including an assessment of popular perceptions of science and technology, see Peter N. Carroll, *It Seemed Like Nothing Happened: America in the 1970s* (New York: Holt, Rinehart and Winston, 1982).

3. For a discussion of those efforts, see Bruce L. R. Smith, *The Advisers: Scientists in the Policy Process* (Washington: The Brookings Institution, 1992). For a concise account of the President's science advisory apparatus,

CHAPTER 1 ENDNOTES

see Detlev W. Bronk, "Science Advice in the White House: The Genesis of the President's Science Advisers and the National Science Foundation," *Science*, 186 (11 October 1974), 116-121 [reprinted in William T. Golden (ed.), *Science Advice to the President* (New York: Pergamon Press, 1980), pp. 245-256].

4. For an overview of these developments, see Stine, *A History of Science Policy in the United States*; and Smith, *American Science Policy since World War II*. For the general issue of advising the Congress on technical matters, see the appropriate essays in William T. Golden (ed.), *Science and Technology Advice to the President, Congress, and Judiciary* (New York: Pergamon Press, 1988); and William G. Wells, Jr., *Working with Congress: A Practical Guide for Scientists and Engineers* (Washington: American Association for the Advancement of Science, 1992). Also useful are *Science and the Congress: The Third Franklin Conference* (Philadelphia: Franklin Institute Press, 1978); and John H. Trattner, *The Prune Book: The 60 Toughest Science and Technology Jobs in Washington* (Lanham, MD: Madison Books, 1992), pp. 476-539.

5. For a general discussion of congressional concern with environmental issues in the late 1960s, see Richard A. Cooley and Geoffrey Wandesforde-Smith (eds.), *Congress and the Environment* (Seattle: University of Washington Press, 1970); Ronald Lee Shelton, "The Environmental Era: A Chronological Guide to Policy and Concepts, 1962-1972," Ph.D. dissertation, Cornell University, 1973; and Lynton K. Caldwell, *Science and the National Environmental Policy Act: Redirecting Policy through Procedural Reform* (University: University of Alabama Press, 1982).

6. Nelson W. Polsby, "Policy Analysis and Congress," *Public Policy*, 28 (Fall 1969), 70-71. Also useful for their contemporary analyses of professional staff capabilities and need for reform are Samuel C. Patterson, "Congressional Committee Professional Staffing: Capabilities and Constraints," in Allan Kornberg and Lloyd D. Musolf (eds.), *Legislatures in Development Perspective* (Durham, NC: Duke University Press, 1970), pp. 391-428; and Susan Webb Hammond, "Characteristics of Congressional Staffers," in James J. Heaphey and Alan P. Balutis (eds.), *Legislative Staffing: A Comparative Perspective* (New York: Sage Publishers, 1975), pp. 60-85. The classic treatment of the growing dominance of the executive branch over the legislative branch is Arthur M. Schlesinger, Jr., *The Imperial Presidency* (Boston: Houghton Mifflin Company, 1973).

7. These concerns were well represented in Jonathan Allen (ed.), *March 4: Scientists, Students, and Society* (Cambridge: The MIT Press, 1970).

8. Board Statement on AAAS Membership, adopted by the AAAS Board of Directors, 19 October 1969 (*AAAS Resolutions*, p. 10; copy in Office of the Executive Officer, AAAS, Washington, D.C.).

9. Philip M. Boffey, "AAAS (I): Facing the Questions of What It Should Be and Do," *Science*, 172 (30 April 1971), 453. [Emphasis in original.]

10. See ibid., pp. 453-456, 458; and Philip M. Boffey, "AAAS (III): Is Order of Magnitude Expansion a Reasonable Goal?" *Science*, 172 (16 May 1971), 656-658. Post-World War II developments within AAAS are most fully recounted in Dael Wolfle, *Renewing a Scientific Society: The American Association for the Advancement of Science from World War II to 1970* (Washington: AAAS, 1989). Also useful is Bruce V. Lewenstein, "The AAAS and Scientific Perspectives on Public Understanding, 1945-1980," paper presented at the AAAS annual meeting, Washington, D.C., 17 February 1991.

11. Quoted in Boffey, "AAAS (III)," p. 656.

12. For the background and early activities of SWOPSI, see Joel Primack and Frank von Hippel, *Advice and Dissent: Scientists in the Political Arena* (New York: Basic Books, 1974), pp. 196-207.

13. This work was initially disseminated in a 21-page pamphlet, *Congress and Technology* (Stanford, CA: Stanford Workshop on Political and Social Issues, Stanford University, April 1970), and in a typescript report, Frank von Hippel and Joel Primack, *The Politics of Technology: Activities and Responsibilities of Scientists in the Direction of Technology* (Stanford, CA: Stanford Workshops on Social and Political Issues, Stanford University, September 1970). Von Hippel and Primack subsequently expanded and revised their report, publishing it as Primack and von Hippel, *Advice and Dissent*.

14. Von Hippel and Primack, *The Politics of Technology*, p. v.

15. Ibid., p. 121.

16. For background of the technology assessment idea, see Carroll Pursell, "Belling the Cat: A Critique of Technology Assessment," *Lex et Scientia*, 10 (Oct.-Dec. 1974), 130-145. Also useful for their insights into the fluid nature of debates surrounding technology assessment at the time are: Louis H. Mayo, "The Relationship of Technology Assessment to Environmental Management," Staff Discussion Paper 206 (Washington: Program of Policy Studies in Science and Technology, George Washington University, October 1969); Raphael G. Kasper, "Some Comments on Technology Assessment and the Environment," Occasional Paper No. 8 (Washington: Program of Policy Studies in Science

Chapter 1 Endnotes

and Technology, George Washington University, November 1970); and Ellis R. Mottur, "Technology Assessment and Environmental Engineering," Occasional Paper No. 9 (Washington: Program of Policy Studies in Science and Technology, George Washington University, November 1970).

17. Von Hippel and Primack, *The Politics of Technology*, p. 130.

18. Analysis of the questionnaire, as well as the tabulated data, are contained in von Hippel and Primack, *The Politics of Technology*, appendix A; and in *Congress and Technology*.

19. Von Hippel and Primack, *The Politics of Technology*, appendix A.

20. Telephone interview, author with Joel R. Primack, 29 September 1993.

21. Quoted in William Bevan to James Reed, 29 January 1973 (Congressional Fellows/1971-73 folder, box 2, Catherine Borras Second Accession collection, AAAS Archives, Washington, D.C. [hereafter cited as "Borras collection"]). The strife evident at the late 1960s AAAS meetings was detailed in telephone interview, author with Richard A. Scribner, 28 September 1993; and telephone interview, author with Alan McGowan, 22 June 1994.

22. McGowan interview, 22 June 1994; Primack interview, 29 September 1993; and Scribner interview, 28 September 1993. McGowan attended the original meeting in December 1969, as the guest of Barry Commoner. Primack was brought in the following year, under the sponsorship of Richard Bolt.

23. Report of the Committee of Young Scientists to the Board of Directors of the AAAS, 7 March 1970 (Congressional Fellows/1971-73 folder, box 2, Borras collection).

24. "Discussion with Emilio Q. Daddario," addition to the minutes of the meeting of the Committee on Science in the Promotion of Human Welfare, 3 April 1971 (BD #1 folder, Board of Directors Minutes, AAAS Archives, Washington, D.C. [hereafter cited as "Board Minutes"]).

25. Joel Primack to Richard Bolt, 14 September 1971 (Congressional Fellows/1971-73 folder, box 2, Borras collection). Bolt, who had been on the AAAS Board of Directors for several years and who was one of the senior scientists supportive of increased social responsibility among scientists and engineers, was a principal in the Cambridge, Mass., engineering firm Bolt Beranek and Newman, Inc.

26. Ibid.

27. Appendix 2 of the Minutes of the 30 September 1971 meeting of the AAAS Committee on Science in the Promotion of Human Welfare (Early CSEFP Material folder, box 1, Claudia Sturges Congressional Fellows collection, AAAS Archives, Washington, D.C. [hereafter cited as "Sturges collection"]).

28. See William Bevan to Walter Modell, 17 November 1971 (Congressional Fellows/1971-73 folder, box 2, Borras collection); and Board of Directors Minutes, 9 October 1971, pp. 6-7 (BD #2 folder, Board Minutes). At that time, Scribner was the son-in-law of AAAS Board of Directors member Richard Bolt.

29. Being new to the world of congressional rules and regulations, the AAAS staff did not yet understand that committee offices in both houses and the personal offices of representatives were limited to a specific number of paid personnel they could retain on their staffs at any one time. Thus, the real appeal of the fellowship program was not the money saved by those congressional offices hosting a Fellow, but the fact that the Fellows enabled the offices to add professional staff members without exceeding their caps on salaried employees.

30. "Some Questions about the AAAS Scientist Intern Program," a list of questions marked "NOT FOR CIRCULATION," dated 20 January 1972 (Early CSEFP Material folder, box 1, Sturges collection). Among other names considered in 1972 were Visiting Scientist in Congress, Scientist-Intern in Congress, and Congressional Scientist-Intern Program.

31. "An American Association for the Advancement of Science Program of Government Internships for Young Scientists," a draft background report labeled "NOT FOR CIRCULATION," dated 8 February 1972 (Early CSEFP Material folder, box 1, Sturges collection).

32. Ibid.

33. Ibid.

34. Ibid.

35. For brief overviews of Congress's access to and evaluation of scientific and technological information, see Richard Barke, *Science, Technology, and Public Policy* (Washington: CQ Press, 1986), pp. 21-42; Jeffrey K. Stine, "Fulfilling the Science and Technology Advisory Needs of Congress," in Golden, *Science and Technology Advice to the President, Congress, and Judiciary*,

pp. 443-446; and Marcel C. LaFollette and Jeffrey K. Stine, "Congressional Hearings on Science and Technology Issues: Strengths, Weaknesses, and Suggested Improvements," background paper prepared for the Committee on Science, Technology, and Congress of the Carnegie Commission on Science, Technology, and Government, 1990.

36. "An American Association for the Advancement of Science Program of Government Internships for Young Scientists."

37. Program costs included the orientation program, advertising, subsidized dinners and lunches for Fellows during the fellowship year, and a percentage of salaries for two AAAS staff members. The AAAS recouped much of these costs through a management fee paid by the participating societies.

38. This was the name used in February 1972. See, for example, Richard A. Scribner to Charles A. Mosher, 28 February 1972 (Congressional Fellows/1971-73 folder, box 2, Borras collection).

39. Ibid.

40. See AAAS Youth Council Meeting Minutes, 28 December 1972 (BD #4 folder, Board Minutes). Scribner elaborated on Primack's persistence in Scribner interview, 28 September 1993. See also, Joel Primack to Richard Scribner, 30 November 1973 (BD #5 folder, Board Minutes).

41. Quoted in "New Program Announced: The ASME Congressional Fellow," *Mechanical Engineering*, 94 (August 1972), 86. For a history of ASME, see Bruce Sinclair, *A Centennial History of the American Society of Mechanical Engineers, 1880-1980* (Toronto: University of Toronto Press, 1980).

42. With a master's degree in chemistry from Washington State University, Mike McCormack distinguished himself as one of the few congressional members with a science background.

43. Telephone interview, author with John Andelin, 30 March 1994 and 4 April 1994; and "New Program Announced."

44. For example, the ASME staff met with Dave Brunell (an electrical engineer working for Representative Donald Riegle), John Andelin (a physicist working for Representative Mike McCormack), and J. Thomas Ratchford (a physicist working for the House Committee on Science and Astronautics). See William P. Miller, Jr., to J. W. Davis, 28 June 1972; and William P. Miller, Jr., to E. H. Walton, 3 August 1972 (ASME folder, box 1, Sturges collection).

45. William P. Miller, Jr., to E. H. Walton, no date [probably late July 1972] (ASME folder, box 1, Sturges collection).

46. "New Program Announced."

47. E. H. Walton to Joel Primack, 30 October 1972 (ASME folder, box 1, Sturges collection).

48. Barry Hyman, "Guest Comment," *Production Engineering*, 20 (June 1973), 13.

49. Golden had expressed his philosophical agreement with Primack's congressional fellowship idea earlier that year. See William T. Golden to Joel Primack, 5 April 1972 (William T. Golden personal files, New York City). Golden discussed the background to his decision in William T. Golden to Michael Telson and Albert H. Teich, 12 August 1987 (William T. Golden personal files); and interview, author with William T. Golden, 21 February 1994.

50. Having promised to provide whatever amount was necessary to launch the congressional fellowship program, Golden ultimately donated $27,500. See William Bevan to William T. Golden, 10 December 1973 (Congressional Fellows/1971-73 folder, box 2, Borras collection). Although AAAS officials had kept Golden's gift anonymous, Joel Primack learned of Golden's intentions through their private conversations and mentioned it in a footnote in Primack and von Hippel, *Advice and Dissent*, p. 281. Conversations between Golden and Primack were discussed in Golden interview, 21 February 1994; and in Primack interview, 29 September 1993. In recalling the series of events leading to the formation of the congressional fellowship program, Golden told Primack: "But for your initiative and persistence the program would not have been started. I also played a role, which would, however, have been of no effect without your earlier initiative and your follow-up." William T. Golden to Joel R. Primack, 14 March 1980 (William T. Golden personal files).

51. William T. Golden to William Drayton, 10 January 1973 (William T. Golden personal files).

52. Memorandum, Bill Drayton to AAASYC Members, 22 January 1973 (William T. Golden personal files).

53. Primack interview, 29 September 1993; Golden interview, 21 February 1994; and telephone interview, author with Michael L. Telson, 9 May 1994. At the top of Primack's list were two 27-year-old Ph.D. candidates:

CHAPTER 1   ENDNOTES

Michael L. Telson of MIT and Jessica Tuchman of Cal Tech, both of whom eventually became members of the first class of AAAS Congressional Fellows.

54. Scribner interview, 28 September 1993.

55. Richard A. Scribner, "Scientist Congressional Fellows," *Science*, 180 (April 13, 1973), 139.

56. William Bevan to James Reed, 29 January 1973 (Congressional Fellows/1971-73 folder, box 2, Borras collection). The Kettering Foundation turned down the AAAS's grant request in 1973, as did the Rockefeller Foundation. See James M. Reed to William Bevan, 20 February 1973; and John H. Knowles to William Bevan, 19 March 1973 (Congressional Fellows/1971-73 folder, box 2, Borras collection).

57. Richard Scribner to David Willis, 20 June 1973 (Congressional Fellows/1971-73 folder, box 2, Borras collection). The Milbank Memorial Fund awarded a special $5,000 grant to the AAAS to assist with the first year's program (see L.E. Burney to Richard Scribner, 24 July 1973 [same folder]), while IBM followed suit with a $3,500 grant (see Lewis M. Branscomb to Richard Scribner, 22 August 1973 [same folder]).

58. William Bevan to Hugh F. Cline, 12 December 1973 (Congressional Fellows/1971-73 folder, box 2, Borras collection). For background to interactions of the AAAS with the Russell Sage Foundation, see William Bevan, memorandum to the file (subj.: Report on visit to the Russell Sage Foundation), 27 March 1973 (Congressional Science Fellows Program/1974-75 Pending folder, box 2, Development Office records, AAAS Archives, Washington, D.C. [hereafter cited as "Development Office records"]).

59. William T. Golden to Mrs. Lester R. [Barbara] Tuchman, 6 May 1974 (Congressional Fellows/1971-73 folder, box 2, Borras collection). This letter represented Golden's unsuccessful attempt to solicit a contribution for the AAAS Congressional Fellowship Program from Barbara Tuchman, whose daughter Jessica (now Jessica Tuchman Mathews) was a member of the first class of AAAS Congressional Fellows.

60. F. Dow Smith to "Dear Member," May 1974 (Congressional Fellows/1971-73 folder, box 2, Borras collection).

61. This program was meant to counter the APSA's long-standing emphasis on the executive branch. For news coverage of the then novel enterprise, see "'Interns' Planned to Serve Congress," *New York Times*, 4 May 1953; "Political Scientists Choose 6 as 'Congressional Interns,'" *Washington*

Post, 22 June 1953; and Abbie and Raymond J. Blair, "Hill 'Interns' Find It's a Busy Grind," *Washington Post*, 1 August 1954.

62. The program eventually expanded to include federal executives (who were sponsored by the U.S. Civil Service Commission) and other professionals. In 1974, for example, the Robert Wood Johnson Foundation established a Health Policy Fellows program, administered by the APSA, which was intended for mid-career academic health professionals.

63. The first year's class began with a two-month orientation, operating out of the Library of Congress, while the 1954 class started the tradition of a one-month training session.

64. Original support for the program came from the Edgar Stern Family Fund. Additional money came later from the Ford Foundation, the Rockefeller Brothers Fund, the New York Times Foundation, the Poynter Fund, and others. For an overview of the APSA fellowship program, see Ronald D. Hedlund, "Participant Observation in Studying Congress: The Congressional Fellowship Program," final report submitted to the Congressional Fellowship Program Advisory Committee, American Political Science Association, 1971 (copy in the Congressional Fellowship Program Office, American Political Science Association, Washington, D.C.); and Mary Ann Larkin, "Congressional Fellows: Helping Congress Help America," *Exxon USA*, 23 (no. 2, 1984), 22-25.

65. Ratchford had earned his Ph.D. in solid state physics at the University of Virginia and had taught at Washington and Lee University before moving to Washington, D.C., in 1964 to accept a "temporary" job at the Air Force Office of Scientific Research. Telephone interview, author with J. Thomas Ratchford, 14 June 1994.

66. See Hedlund, "Participant Observation in Studying Congress," p. 1. Westman, an ecologist from Cornell University, spent a significant part of his fellowship working on water legislation for the Senate Air and Water Pollution Subcommittee.

67. Ibid., passim.

68. Scribner interview, 28 September 1993.

69. Arthur H. Purcell, undated press release on the AAAS Congressional Scientist-Fellowship Program [probably June 1973], (CSFP/Ads and Announcements of Program folder, 1973-74 publicity file, box M-U-Z #1, CSEFP 1973-1978 records, AAAS Archives, Washington, D.C.)

Chapter 2

1. Memorandum, Richard Scribner and Arthur Purcell to William Bevan, 17 July 1973 (Congressional Fellows/1971-73 folder, box 2, Catherine Borras Second Accession collection, AAAS Archives, Washington, D.C. [hereafter cited as "Borras collection"]).

2. See memorandum, Richard Scribner and Arthur Purcell to William Bevan, 17 July 1973; and Richard Scribner to William T. Golden, 18 May 1973 (Congressional Fellows/1971-73 folder, box 2, Borras collection). The high number of applications from physicists was undoubtedly stimulated by the promotional effort associated with the American Physical Society's concurrently launched fellowship program. AAAS received 92 applications for the second year (1974-75), again from across the scientific disciplines and engineering (see memorandum, Richard Scribner to William Bevan, 19 April 1974 [same folder]).

3. See Appendix B: Favorable Congressional Responses to the AAAS Congressional Scientist-Fellow Program [undated; probably September 1973] (1973-74 CSFP Congressional Survey folder, 1973-74 CSFP correspondence file, box M-U-2 #6, CSEFP 1973-78 records, AAAS Archives, Washington, D.C. [hereafter cited as "CSEFP records"]); and Scribner and Purcell to Bevan, 17 July 1973.

4. Henry M. Jackson to Richard Scribner, 14 May 1973 (1973-74 CSFP Congressional Survey folder, 1973-74 CSFP correspondence file, box M-U-2 #6, CSEFP records).

5. See Richard Scribner to William T. Golden, 18 May 1973 (Congressional Fellows/1971-83 folder, box 2, Borras collection).

6. See, for example, Richard Scribner to William T. Golden, 18 May 1973 (Congressional Fellows/1971-73 folder, box 2, Borras collection).

7. Walter E. Beach to Richard A. Scribner, 15 October 1973 (Congressional Fellows/1971-73 folder, box 2, Borras collection). For Beach's continuing efforts to persuade AAAS to reconsider the name of its fellowship program, see Walter E. Beach to Richard Scribner, 19 November 1973 (same folder).

8. Telephone interview, author with Richard A. Scribner, 28 September 1993; and telephone interview, author with Michael L. Telson, 9 May 1994.

9. Information on these Fellows is drawn primarily from a summary of the first fellowship class in the Congressional Fellows/1971-73 folder, box 2, Borras collection; and from final reports submitted by the Fellows (all in the Summary Data/1973-74 binder, box 1, CSEFP Summary Data records, AAAS Archives, Washington, D.C. [hereafter cited as "Summary Data records"]). Data on the Congressional Science and Engineering Fellows through 1992 may be found in *Directory of AAAS Science and Engineering Fellows, 1973-92* (Washington: AAAS, 1992). An updated version of the directory will be published in late 1994. See also, John Wilkinson, Jr., *Congressional Science and Engineering Fellows Program Evaluation* (Washington: AAAS, 1993).

10. In 1977, the committee gained new jurisdictions that were reflected in its new name—Committee on Energy and Natural Resources.

11. For a description of his fellowship year, see Benjamin S. Cooper and N. Richard Werthamer, "Two Physicists on Capitol Hill," *Physics Today*, 28 (January 1975), 63-66.

12. For a description of his fellowship year, see ibid.

13. Tuchman, daughter of the acclaimed historian Barbara Tuchman, later married, adding the last name Mathews.

14. Scribner first met Hyman in spring 1973 when Scribner was canvassing Congress for offices willing to host one or more of the AAAS/APS/IEEE Fellows who would arrive in September. Scribner interview, 28 September 1993.

15. See, for example, Richard A. Scribner to William Miller, 26 April 1974 (ASME folder, box 1, Claudia Sturges Congressional Fellows collection, AAAS Archives, Washington, D.C. [hereafter cited as "Sturges collection"]).

16. Richard Scribner to Rogers B. Finch, 10 February 1976 (Congressional Fellows/1971-73 folder, box 2, Borras collection).

17. See Arleen Richman, memorandum to the files, 25 January 1980 (ASME folder, box 1, Sturges collection).

18. For a discussion of the first class of Fellows and the early impact of the program, see Constance Holden, "Science Fellows in Washington: From Lab Work to Legislation," *Science*, 189 (September 12, 1975), 860-862. Richard

CHAPTER 2 ENDNOTES

Werthamer was the only Fellow who did not accept a paid congressional staff position, choosing instead to return to his former employer, Bell Laboratories.

19. Henry M. Jackson to Richard A. Scribner, 11 June 1974 (Congressional Responses/1975 binder, Congressional Response Forms/1973-80 box, Sturges collection). For an overview of congressional responses to the energy crisis, see James Everett Katz, *Congress and National Energy Policy* (New Brunswick, NJ: Transaction Books, 1984).

20. For brief discussions of the Arab oil embargo, see Martin V. Melosi, *Coping with Abundance: Energy and Environment in Industrial America* (Philadelphia: Temple University Press, 1985), pp. 278-286; Daniel Yergin, *The Prize: The Epic Quest for Oil, Money, and Power* (New York: Simon & Schuster, 1991), pp. 588-619; and Thomas W. Lippman, "Memories of Gas Lines Dimmed by Time and Tide of Oil," *Washington Post* (26 November 1993). For the influence of the energy crisis on the assignments of some of the early congressional Fellows, see Allan Hoffman, Thomas Moss, and Haven Whiteside, "Helping Shape Legislative Policy," *Physics Today*, 30 (August 1977), 42-48.

21. Although Andelin had offered to volunteer, he was paid the minimal salary for practical purposes—so that he could be issued an identification badge and keys to the office. Telephone interview, author with John Andelin, 30 March 1994.

22. For a discussion of the Task Force on Energy and the Subcommittee on Energy, see Ken Hechler, *Toward the Endless Frontier: History of the Committee on Science and Technology, 1959-79* (Washington: GPO, 1980), pp. 655-693.

23. See Mike McCormack to Richard A. Scribner, 23 May 1974 (Congressional Responses/1975 binder, Congressional Response Forms/1973-80 box, Sturges collection).

24. For principal issues addressed by presidential science advisors, see William T. Golden (ed.), *Science Advice to the President* (New York: Pergamon Press, 1980); William T. Golden (ed.), *Science and Technology Advice to the President, Congress, and Judiciary* (New York: Pergamon Press, 1988); Gregg Herken, *Cardinal Choices: Presidential Science Advising from the Atomic Bomb to SDI* (New York: Oxford University Press, 1992); and Zuoyue Wang, "American Science and the Cold War: The Rise of the President's Science Advisory Committee, 1950-1961," Ph.D. dissertation, University of California, Santa Barbara, 1994.

25. There were a few exceptions such as Thomas E. Cooper, the 1975-76 American Society of Mechanical Engineers Fellow who worked for the House Committee on Armed Services, and Alton G. Keel, Jr., the 1977-78 American Institute of Aeronautics and Astronautics Fellow who worked for the Senate Committee on Armed Services, yet the vast majority of Fellows contributed to areas outside of national security.

26. Holden, "Science Fellows in Washington," p. 860.

27. See memorandum, Allan Hoffman to Mary Shoaf and Richard Scribner, 2 September 1975 (Summary Data/1974-75 binder, box 1, Summary Data records).

28. See Lloyd B. Craine to Richard Scribner, 16 October 1975 (Summary Data/1974-75 binder, box 1, Summary Data records).

29. See Melosi, *Coping with Abundance*, pp. 307-308; and Katz, *Congress and National Energy Policy*, pp. 38-39, 224-226.

30. See Dilys M. Hill, "Domestic Policy," in M. Glenn Abernathy, Dilys M. Hill, and Phil Williams (eds.), *The Carter Years: The President and Policy Making* (New York: St. Martin's Press, 1984), pp. 14-19.

31. For a detailed history of the committee, see Hechler, *Toward the Endless Frontier*. The committee only had jurisdiction over civilian R&D within ERDA.

32. For discussions of changes that occurred within the Science Committee, see Lloyd B. Craine to Richard Scribner, 16 October 1975 (Summary Data/1974-75 binder, box 1, Summary Data records); and interview, author with John D. Holmfeld, 8 September 1993.

33. Thomas Moss to Richard Scribner and Mary Shoaf, 20 October 1975 (Summary Data/1974-75 binder, box 1, Summary Data records).

34. Haven Whiteside, Report on Congressional Fellowship, 24 September 1975 (Summary Data/1974-75 binder, box 1, Summary Data records).

35. Richard Scribner to William Havens, Jr., 18 June 1973 (American Physical Society folder, Misc. Congressional and Diplomacy Program active files, Directorate for Science and Policy Programs, AAAS, Washington, D.C. [hereafter cited as "CDP active files"]). This letter to APS's executive secretary outlines AAAS's plans for the first year's fellowship orientation.

CHAPTER 2 ENDNOTES

36. Detailed agendas from every orientation program are kept in the working files of the AAAS Directorate for Science and Policy Programs. Representatives from the following executive branch agencies usually addressed each new class of Fellows: Office of Management and Budget, Department of Defense, Department of State, National Science Foundation, and National Institutes of Health. As the fellowship program matured, former Fellows assumed important roles as speakers at the orientation sessions.

37. Interview, author with Albert H. Teich, 21 September 1993. The opportunity to speak before a whole group of Fellows (as opposed to one or two at a time) no doubt improved the ability of AAAS to attract influential people to make presentations during the orientation period.

38. Chuck Blahous, End of the Year Report, 31 July 1990 (1989-90 Science and Engineering Fellows Summary binder, CDP active files).

39. Scribner interview, 28 September 1993.

40. These seminars typically were guided by a representative set of each year's Fellows who selected topics and speakers in consultation with the AAAS staff, who handled the logistical elements.

41. Richard A. Scribner to Rogers B. Finch, 10 February 1976 (Congressional Fellows/1971-73 folder, box 2, Borras collection).

42. William T. Golden to Mrs. Lester R. [Barbara] Tuchman, 6 May 1974 (Congressional Fellows/1971-73 folder, box 2, Borras collection).

43. Golden's 1974 gift was for $8,500. See William T. Golden to Michael Telson and Albert H. Teich, 12 August 1987 (William T. Golden personal files, New York City).

44. For purposes of its own records and public dissemination, AAAS referred to those six OTA Fellows funded by the Ford Foundation grant as AAAS Congressional Fellows. Later, beginning in 1978, a category of OTA Congressional Fellows was added, these Fellows being wholly sponsored by OTA and put through the administrative program of AAAS.

45. N. Richard Werthamer to Leonard M. Rieser, Jr., 14 June 1974 (Congressional Fellows/1971-73 folder, box 2, Borras collection).

Chapter 3

1. William Bevan to Albert Bandura, 2 April 1974 (American Psychological Association folder, box 1, Claudia Sturges Congressional Fellows collection, AAAS Archives, Washington, D.C. [hereafter cited as "Sturges collection"]).

2. See memorandum, Richard Scribner to William Bevan, 20 June 1974 (Congressional Fellows/1971-73 folder, box 2, Catherine Borras Second Accession collection, AAAS Archives, Washington, D.C. [hereafter cited as "Borras collection"]). Ebert later married and added the surname Flattau. Other members of the class of 1974-75 included Kevin Cornell (AAAS-Rockefeller), who worked for Senator Gary Hart; Lloyd Craine (IEEE), who worked for the House Committee on Science and Technology; Jerome Harper (AAAS), who worked for OTA; Allan Hoffman (APS), who worked for the Environment Subcommittee of the Senate Committee on Commerce; Thomas Moss (APS), who worked for Representative George E. Brown, Jr.; Willis Smith (IEEE), who worked for the Senate Committee on Interior and Insular Affairs; Haven Whiteside (APS), who worked for the Subcommittee on Air and Water Pollution of the Senate Committee on Public Works; and William Widnall (AIAA), who worked for the House Committee on Science and Technology.

3. See Lawrence Froman, Congressional Fellowship Program Final Report, 13 September 1976 (Summary Data 1975-76 binder, box 1, CSEFP Summary Data records, AAAS Archives, Washington, D.C. [hereafter cited as "Summary Data records"]).

4. Memorandum, Richard Scribner to William Bevan, 20 June 1974 (Congressional Fellows/1971-73 folder, box 2, Borras collection).

5. "Senate Concurrent Resolution 100—Expression of Appreciation to Various Professional Societies for Their Congressional Science and Engineering Fellowship Programs," *Congressional Record—Senate*, 122 (March 10, 1976), 3116. See also, Mary C. Dolan, "Congress Praises Fellows Program," *Science*, 192 (May 7, 1976), 554-555.

6. "Senate Concurrent Resolution 100," p. 3115. Kennedy had firsthand experience that year with Arthur M. Silverstein, a Federation of American Societies for Experimental Biology congressional Fellow assigned to the Senate Subcommittee on Health. Kennedy's $1 million figure represented the combined compensation Fellows could have commanded, had

CHAPTER 3   ENDNOTES

Congress hired them, not the actual sum of their fellowship stipends. Several scientists and engineers had taken salary cuts to serve as Fellows.

7. Ibid. Glenn had hosted the 1975-76 AAAS Congressional Fellow, David W. Hafemeister, in his personal office.

8. William Bevan to Donald T. Campbell, 5 March 1975 (American Psychological Association folder, box 1, Sturges collection). Richard Scribner recalled that all of the participating societies wrestled at one time or another with the same internal conflict over how best to expend their resources: trying deliberately to influence Congress on behalf of their discipline or working to fulfill their social responsibility by offering a public service through the fellowship program. For some organizations such as the American Psychological Association, American Chemical Society, and American Society of Mechanical Engineers, this tension was especially strong. Telephone interview, author with Richard A. Scribner, 28 September 1993.

9. For the work of later APA Congressional Fellows, see Patrick H. DeLeon, Robinsue Frohboese, and Judith C. Meyers, "Psychologist on Capitol Hill: A Unique Use of the Skills of the Scientist/Practitioner," *Professional Psychology: Research and Practice*, 15 (no. 5, 1984), 697-705; and Henry Saeman, "Two APA Science Fellows Vow to Make Impact," *The Ohio Psychologist*, 34 (April 1988), 18-19.

10. William D. Carey to Robert N. Kreidler, 6 August 1975 (Sloan Foundation/1976-77 folder, box 2, Development Office records, AAAS Archives, Washington, D.C. [hereafter cited as "Development Office records"]). The importance of avoiding conflicts of interest was stressed from the very first class of Fellows. See Ronal W. Larson, Final Report to the IEEE, May 1974 (Summary Data/1973-74 binder, box 1, Summary Data records).

11. Golden asked that his $28,000 gift be extended over two fellowship years, which it was. See William T. Golden to William D. Carey, 1 October 1976 and William D. Carey to William T. Golden, 14 October 1976 (William T. Golden Foundation/1976 folder, box 2, Development Office records).

12. See William D. Carey to Julius Bergen, 23 November 1976 (Fleischmann Proposal folder, box 1, Sturges collection).

13. AAAS grant application to the Max C. Fleischmann Foundation for support of a Program of Science and Engineering Fellows with Congress, November 10, 1976 (Fleischmann Proposal folder, box 1, Sturges collection).

14. Interview, author with Stephen D. Nelson, 21 September 1993.

15. Ibid. Nelson assumed program leadership in 1984.

16. AAAS Office of Science and Society Programs, "The Congressional Science and Engineering Fellow Program of the American Association for the Advancement of Science," October 1974 (copy in 1973-74 Selection Committee folder, 1973-74 selection files, box M-U-2 #1, CSEFP 1973-78 records, AAAS Archives, Washington, D.C. [hereafter cited as "CSEFP records"]).

17. See "Eck, Ziman Complete Year as ACS Fellows," *Chemical and Engineering News*, 58 (October 27, 1980), 34.

18. Walter Ellis quoted in minutes, 13 December 1979 meeting of representatives of societies sponsoring Congressional Science and Engineering Fellows (Participating Societies Meetings/1981-82 folder, box 27, Sturges collection).

19. Minutes of 23 June 1980 meeting of representatives of organizations participating in the Congressional Science and Engineering Fellowship Program (Participating Societies Meetings/1981-82 folder, box 27, Sturges collection). For an extended discussion of the "two cultures" idea, see C. P. Snow, *The Two Cultures* (Cambridge: Cambridge University Press, 1993), which contains Snow's original 1959 essay and his 1963 follow-up essay, as well as a splendid 66-page introduction by Stefan Collini.

20. J. Thomas Ratchford to W.W. Havens, Jr., 3 June 1980 (American Physical Society folder, Misc. Congressional and Diplomacy Program active files, Directorate for Science and Policy Programs, AAAS, Washington, D.C. [hereafter cited as "CDP active files"]).

21. Richard A. Scribner, memorandum for the record, 6 July 1981 (American Physical Society folder, CDP active files).

22. Joseph C. Cain to Richard Scribner, 24 November 1976 (American Geophysical Union folder, box 1, Sturges collection).

23. See A. F. Spilhaus, Jr. to Richard Scribner, 27 December 1976 (American Geophysical Union folder, box 1, Sturges collection).

24. Steve Nelson, memorandum to the file, 26 May 1989 (23 May 1990 folder, Society Representatives' Meetings files, CDP active files).

CHAPTER 4 ENDNOTES

25. Richard Krasnow, Year End Report, no date [probably September 1982] (Summary Data/1981-82 binder, box 1, Summary Data records).

Chapter 4

1. Telephone interview, author with William T. Golden, 29 June 1994.

2. Joel Primack, Proposal for American Physical Society sponsorship of a Congressional Fellow in 1973-74, submitted to the APS Council, no date [probably March or April 1973] (copy in APS Congressional Fellow/Early Material folder, box 1, Claudia Sturges Congressional Fellows collection, AAAS Archives, Washington, D.C. [hereafter cited as "Sturges collection"]).

3. Other committee members were John Andelin, Anne H. Cahn, Joel R. Primack, and Richard A. Scribner.

4. Committee on Congressional Fellowships, APS Forum on Physics and Society, "A Proposal for a Congressional Science Fellowship Program for Physicists," 11 January 1973 (copy in APS Congressional Fellow/Early Material folder, box 1, Sturges collection).

5. See Barry M. Casper to APS Committee on Congressional Fellowships, 20 February 1973 (APS Congressional Fellow/Early Material folder, box 1, Sturges collection).

6. W.W. Havens, Jr., to Barry M. Casper, 4 April 1973 (APS Congressional Fellow/Early Material folder, box 1, Sturges collection).

7. Barry M. Casper to Audrey Armstrong, 9 April 1973 (APS Congressional Fellow/Early Material folder, box 1, Sturges collection).

8. See "The American Physical Society Congressional Fellowship Program," *Bulletin of the American Physical Society*, 18 (June 1973), 842.

9. For an early indication of APS's importance, see memorandum, Richard Scribner and Arthur Purcell to William Bevan, 17 July 1973 (Congressional Fellows/1971-73 folder, box 2, Catherine Borras Second Accession collection, AAAS Archives, Washington, D.C. [hereafter cited as "Borras collection"]). Also stressed in telephone interview, author with Richard A. Scribner, 28 September 1993.

10. Harold L. Davis, "Needed: More Physicists on the Hill," *Physics Today*, 26 (November 1973), 88.

11. Ibid.

12. Ibid.

13. See memorandum, Richard Scribner to William Bevan, 14 March 1974 (Congressional Fellows/1971-73 folder, box 2, Borras collection). For a self-described summary of experiences of first two Fellows, see Benjamin S. Cooper and N. Richard Werthamer, "Two Physicists on Capitol Hill," *Physics Today*, 28 (January 1975), 63-66.

14. See William A. Fowlder to Richard Scribner, 29 April 1974 (American Physical Society folder, Misc. Congressional and Diplomacy Program active files, Directorate for Science and Policy Programs, AAAS, Washington, D.C. [hereafter cited as "CDP active files"]). The three APS Fellows for 1974-75 collaborated in describing their congressional experiences, all of which dealt with aspects of energy policy. See Allan Hoffman, Thomas Moss, and Haven Whiteside, "Helping Shape Legislative Policy," *Physics Today*, 30 (August 1977), 42-48.

15. Such formal reviews, conducted by internal ad hoc review panels, were conducted in 1978, 1987, and 1991, and are available in the archives of the American Physical Society.

16. Copies of all the "retrospective reviews" of the APS Congressional Fellowship Program are maintained in the Misc. Congressional and Diplomacy Program active files of the AAAS Directorate for Science and Policy Programs.

17. Richard A. Scribner to Joseph A. Burton, 4 November 1976 (American Physical Society folder, CDP active files).

18. Memorandum, Mildred S. Dresselhaus to Members of the Council of the American Physical Society, 2 April 1987 (American Physical Society office files, New York, NY [hereafter cited as "APS files"]).

19. Ibid.

20. Ibid.

21. Ibid.

CHAPTER 4 ENDNOTES

22. Ibid.

23. Memorandum, Ernest M. Henley to Members of the Council of the American Physical Society, 8 October 1991 (APS files).

24. "New Program Announced: The IEEE Congressional Fellow," *IEEE Spectrum*, 10 (January 1973), 8. For a history of IEEE, see A. Michal McMahon, *The Making of a Profession: A Century of Electrical Engineering in America* (New York: IEEE Press, 1984).

25. "IEEE Congressional Fellow Guidelines," no date (attached to J.E. Casey's letter to A. Purcell, 26 April 1973; IEEE folder, box 1, Sturges collection). See also, "IEEE's Congressional Fellow Program—How It Began and How It Operates," *IEEE Spectrum*, 13 (November 1976), 59.

26. For a discussion of the first three years of the IEEE Congressional Engineering Fellowship Program, see Ellis Rubinstein, "EEs Inside Congress," *IEEE Spectrum*, 13 (November 1976), 58-61.

27. P. Gene Smith, Final Report on the IEEE Congressional Fellowship Program, 27 January 1981 (Summary Data/1979-80 binder, CSEFP Summary Data records, AAAS Archives, Washington, D.C. [hereafter cited as "Summary Data records"]).

28. For a history of ACS, see Herman Skolnik and Kenneth M. Reese, *A Century of Chemistry: The Role of Chemists and the American Chemical Society* (Washington: American Chemical Society, 1976).

29. Herman S. Bloch to Alan C. Nixon, 25 April 1973 (Congressional Fellowship Program/1974-75 folder, Committee records, Office of Government Relations active files, American Chemical Society [ACS], Washington, D.C.).

30. See Charles G. Overberger to William J. Bailey, 1 May 1973 (Congressional Fellowship Program/1974-75 folder, Committee records, Office of Government Relations active files, ACS).

31. Memorandum, S. T. Quigley to R. W. Cairns, 25 May 1973 (Congressional Fellowship Program/1974-75 folder, Committee records, Office of Government Relations active files, ACS).

32. Telephone interview, author with Stephen T. Quigley, 13 April 1994.

33. Richard A. Scribner to William T. Golden, 17 September 1973 (Congressional Fellows/1971-73 folder, box 2, Borras collection).

34. Wesley D. Bonds, Jr., to Bernard Friedman, 21 August 1974 (Congressional Fellowship Program/1974-75 folder, Committee records, Office of Government Relations active files, ACS).

35. American Chemical Society Department of Chemistry and Public Affairs, "Proposal for ACS Chemistry and Public Affairs Fellowship Program," no date [probably November 1973] (Congressional Fellowship Program/1974-75 folder, Committee records, Office of Government Relations active files, ACS).

36. The title was changed four years later to the American Chemical Society Congressional Fellows program. See David Hanson, "Althuis Completes Year as ACS Fellow," *Chemical & Engineering News*, 57 (October 15, 1979), 36-37.

37. See Stephen T. Quigley to Renee G. Naves, 27 February 1975 (Congressional Fellowship Program/1974-75 folder, Committee records, Office of Government Relations active files, ACS); and "First Public Affairs Fellow Appointed," *Chemical & Engineering News*, 53 (March 31, 1975), 29.

38. For an example of the ACS staff's efforts to negotiate placements for Naves, see Stephen T. Quigley to Charles Adams Mosher, 29 May 1975 (Congressional Fellowship Program/1974-75 folder, Committee records, Office of Government Relations active files, ACS).

39. Holden, "Science Fellows in Washington," p. 861.

40. See ibid.

41. Minutes of meeting of scientific and engineering society representatives on the subject of Congressional Science and Engineering Fellows, 14 August 1975 [prepared by R. A. Scribner and L. Parfitt on 30 September 1975] (Congressional Fellows/1971-73 folder, box 2, Borras collection); and Quigley interview, 13 April 1994.

42. "Second Public Affairs Fellow Praises Program," *Chemical & Engineering News*, 55 (February 14, 1977), 33.

43. Hanson, "Althuis Completes Year as ACS Fellow." See also, Annette T. Rosenblum and Mary L. Wolfe, "Congressional Fellows," *Chemtech*, 16 (January 1986), 16-20; and "ACS Congressional Fellowship," announcement

distributed by American Chemical Society's Department of Government Relations and Science Policy in 1988 (copy in American Chemical Society folder, ACS file, CDP active files).

44. See Annette T. Rosenblum to Erica Scurr, 8 March 1978 (Congressional Fellowship Program/1974-75 folder, Committee records, Office of Government Relations active files, ACS); and Quigley interview, 13 April 1994.

45. Thomas H. Althuis to Robert A. Alberty, 24 January 1980 (Summary Data/1978-79 binder, box 1, Summary Data records).

46. See minutes of ACS Congressional Fellows meeting, attached to Annette T. Rosenblum, memorandum to ACS Congressional Fellows, 30 September 1983 (Congressional Fellowship Subcommittee/1989 folder, Committee records, Office of Government Relations active files, ACS).

47. Concerns about these developments were expressed among the staff of the ACS's Department of Government Relations and Science Policy. See memorandum, Eric [Leber] to Kathi [Kathleen A. Ream], 23 January 1985 (Congressional Fellowship Background Information folder, Committee records, Office of Government Relations active files, ACS).

48. Rosenblum and Wolfe, "Congressional Fellows," p. 16.

49. See, for example, "First Public Affairs Fellow Appointed"; "Second Public Affairs Fellow Praises Program"; "Brubaker Third Fellow," *Chemical & Engineering News*, 55 (February 14, 1977), 95; "Watts Named ACS Fellow," *Chemical & Engineering News*, 56 (January 16, 1978), 41; Hanson, "Althuis Completes Year as ACS Fellow"; "Eck, Ziman Complete Year as ACS Fellows," *Chemical & Engineering News*, 58 (October 27, 1980), 34-35; "Garin, Greene Complete Year as ACS Fellows," *Chemical & Engineering News*, 59 (September 14, 1981), 58-59; "Barker, Ramonas Enthusiastic about Year's Service as ACS Fellows," *Chemical & Engineering News*, 60 (November 29, 1982), 29-39; and Janice Long, "ACS Has Two New Congressional Fellows," *Chemical & Engineering News*, 63 (November 4, 1985), 42.

50. Rosenblum and Wolfe, "Congressional Fellows," p. 16.

51. William D. Carey to John K Crum, 4 December 1985 (American Chemical Society folder, ACS file, CDP files).

52. John K Crum to William D. Carey, 10 January 1986 (American Chemical Society folder, ACS file, CDP active files).

53. Steve Nelson, memorandum to Rich Nicholson, 12 October 1989 (American Chemical Society folder, ACS file, CDP active files).

54. Ibid.

55. John K Crum to Richard Nicholson, 31 October 1989 (Congressional Fellowship Subcommittee/1989 folder, Committee records, Office of Government Relations active files, ACS). See also, Ernest L. Eliel to Robert A. Roe, 10 January 1990 (American Chemical Society folder, ACS file, CDP active files).

56. Richard S. Nicholson to John K Crum, 3 November 1989 (Congressional Fellowship Program/1990 folder, Committee records, Office of Government Relations active files, ACS). [Emphasis in original.]

57. Albert Gore, Jr., to Clayton F. Callis, 30 November 1989 (CCPA Congressional Fellowship Praises folder, Committee records, Office of Government Relations active files, ACS). For excerpts from letters of support that eventually came forward, including the one from Gore, see John Wiesenfeld, "Opportunity of a Lifetime," *Chemical & Engineering News*, 70 (December 14, 1992), 54. See also, Steve Nelson to Rich Nicholson, 20 October 1989 (American Chemical Society folder, ACS file, CDP active files).

58. Clayton F. Callis to Albert Gore, Jr., 11 December 1989 (Congressional Fellowship Program/1990 folder, Committee records, Office of Government Relations active files, ACS). The exhibition mentioned by Callis, "Science in American Life," was to be a 12,000-square-foot permanent exhibition in the National Museum of American History. ACS agreed to underwrite the project in summer 1989, its $5.5 million contribution becoming the largest single gift for an exhibition ever received by the Smithsonian Institution. See Jeffrey K. Stine, "Planning for Smithsonian's 'Science in American Life' Exhibit under Way," *The Capital Chemist*, 40 (Aug.-Sept. 1990), 30-31; and Linda Romaine Ross, "Science in American Life," *Chemical & Engineering News*, 72 (March 7, 1994), 30-44.

59. Among the issues listed were the belief that ACS did not "benefit sufficiently" from the fellowship program; that the Fellows did not have "sufficient impact" in influencing legislation; and that "ACS does not receive sufficient recognition" because of the prevailing image of the enterprise being a "AAAS Fellows Program." The report concluded that, while the Fellows program had no vocal opponents, neither did it have many "vocal and effective advocates." See Christopher T. Hill, "American Chemical Society Committee on Chemistry and Public Affairs Ad Hoc Probe on the Congressional

Fellowship," unpublished report, 21 August 1990 (copy in Congressional Fellowship Subcommittee/1989 folder, Committee records, Office of Government Relations active files, ACS).

60. See Patricia A. Cunniff to Claudia Sturges, 27 August 1991 (American Chemical Society folder, ACS file, CDP active files); and John Wiesenfeld, "Congressional Fellowship—Opportunity of a Lifetime," *Chemical & Engineering News*, 69 (November 11, 1991), 44.

61. See Patricia A. Cunniff, "ACS Congressional Fellowship Program," a presentation before the [ACS] Committee on Public Affairs & Public Relations, 22 August 1991 (copy in American Chemical Society folder, ACS file, CDP active files).

62. The OTA was established by Public Law 92-484. Among the best studies of OTA are E.B. Skolnikoff, "The Office of Technology Assessment," in Commission on the Operation of the Senate, *Congressional Support Agencies: A Compilation of Papers*, 94th Cong., 2nd sess. (Washington: GPO, 1976), pp. 55-74; U.S. House of Representatives, Committee on Science and Technology, Subcommittee on Science, Research and Technology, *Review of the Office of Technology Assessment and Its Organic Act*, 95th Cong., 2nd sess. (Washington: GPO, 1978); Nancy Carson, "Process, Prescience, and Pragmatism: The Office of Technology Assessment," in Carol H. Weiss (ed.), *Organizations for Policy Analysis: Helping Government Think* (Newbury Park, CA: Sage Publications, 1992), pp. 236-251; and Bruce A. Bimber, "Institutions and Information: The Politics of Expertise in Congress," Ph.D. dissertation, MIT, 1992.

63. For example, see Ronal W. Larson, Final Report to the IEEE, May 1974 (Summary Data/1973-74 binder, Summary Data records).

64. Telephone interview, author with John Andelin, 30 March 1994 and 4 April 1994.

65. For example, see Richard A. Scribner to Emilio Q. Daddario, 31 January 1974 (OTA folder, box 1, Sturges collection).

66. Emilio Q. Daddario to Richard A. Scribner, 7 February 1974 (OTA folder, box 1, Sturges collection).

67. See memorandum, William Bevan to Fran Freeman, Richard Scribner, and Jeannette Wedel, 13 February 1974 (Ford Foundation/1974-75 folder, box 2, Development Office records, AAAS Archives, Washington, D.C. [hereafter cited as "Development Office records"]).

68. "New Scientists with Policy Expertise," *Ford Foundation Letter*, 5 (June 15, 1974), 4.

69. Holden, "Science Fellows in Washington," p. 861.

70. Howard R. Dressner to William Bevan, 19 April 1974 (Congressional Fellows/1971-73 folder, box 2, Borras collection).

71. Jerome Paul Harper, Final Report, 28 August 1975 (Summary Data/1974-75 binder, box 1, Summary Data records).

72. Gary Thomas to Richard Scribner, 25 August 1975 (Summary Data/1974-75 folder, Summary Data records).

73. Telephone interview, author with William Norris, 13 June 1994.

74. Andelin interview, 30 March 1994 and 4 April 1994; Norris interview, 13 June 1994; and telephone interview, author with Nancy Carson, 15 June 1994.

75. Norris interview, 13 June 1994.

76. Andelin interview, 30 March 1994 and 4 April 1994.

77. Norris interview, 13 June 1994. Norris added that OTA has also hired professional staff who had previously been unsuccessful candidates for OTA fellowships and that it has also hired people who had served as Congressional Science and Engineering Fellows under the sponsorship of another non-OTA program.

78. Ibid.

79. William Bevan to Philip Sapir, 4 January 1977 (Child Policy Fellowships folder, box 27, Sturges collection).

80. Philip Sapir to Richard A. Scribner, 3 March 1977 (Child Policy Fellowships folder, box 27, Sturges collection).

81. That grant, which included stipend and administrative expenses, totaled $75,000. See Jane Dustan to Richard A. Scribner, 5 July 1977 (Foundation for Child Development Correspondence folder, box 27, Sturges collection).

82. See Philip Sapir to Richard A. Scribner, 7 July 1978 (W.T. Grant Foundation folder, box 27, Sturges collection). The first four child development

Fellows were Donna L. Chmielewski, Anne H. Cohn Donnelly, Karabelle Pizzigati, and Jack McIver Weatherford.

83. Alberta E. Siegel to William G. Wells, Jr., 14 November 1979 (SRCD Selection folder, box 1, Sturges collection).

84. See William G. Wells, Jr., memorandum to files (subj.: 11 April 1980 meeting with SRCD officials), no date [probably mid-April 1980] (SRCD Fellows Correspondence folder, box 27, Sturges collection).

85. Karen Fischer, memorandum to Jane Dustan, Steve Hersh, Luis Laosa, and Bill Wells, 15 May 1980 (SRCD Fellows Correspondence folder, box 27, Sturges collection). See also, Karen Fischer, memorandum to 1980-81 Congressional Science Fellows in Child Development, 15 May 1980 (same folder).

86. Deborah Phillips, "Financing of the AAAS Congressional Science Fellows: Report of Interviews with Sponsoring Societies," draft, 10 November 1987 (copy in Society for Research in Child Development folder, CDP active files).

87. The rationale, agenda, and evolution of the public history movement can be assessed most easily by perusing its quarterly journal, *The Public Historian*, which began publication in 1979.

88. American Philosophical Association and American Historical Association, "Joint Proposal to the Andrew W. Mellon Foundation for a Program of Congressional Fellowships," 15 August 1979 (Congressional Fellowship Program/Grant folder, American Historical Association office files, Washington, D.C. [hereafter cited as "AHA files"]).

89. Ibid. In making the case for special contributions the two disciplines offered Congress, the associations argued: "The historian brings a concern for an informed humanistic perspective on important social problems. The awareness of the origins and development of a problem, of the solutions that have been tried in the past, and of the relation between a problem and its broader human context can prove to be of vital importance in reaching an informed and sensible proposal for action (and for heading off unsound policies).... Philosophers bring an awareness of the often unexpressed beliefs concerning values present in what appear to be purely technical decisions, and a commitment to the analysis of complicated issues. Disclosing hidden value assumptions and probing arguments for strengths and weaknesses can

contribute to better decisions and to the development of better ways of making decisions."

90. See John E. Sawyer to Mack Thompson, 4 October 1979 (Congressional Fellowship/Grant folder, AHA files).

91. By 1980, there were special break-out sessions on energy, social sciences issues, child policy, and ethical issues. See Arleen Richman, memorandum to the files (subj.: February 5 Meeting with Bill Wells and Mack Thompson) [undated; probably early February 1980] (AHA/APA folder, box 1, Sturges collection). For the contributions of the philosopher fellows, see Milton Coleman, "Philosophy as a Way of Life: For Some Fellows, the Hill Is a Place to Stay," *Washington Post*, 13 June 1986.

92. Memorandum, Melvin Kranzberg to AHA Committee on Congressional Fellowship Program, 11 February 1983 (AHA Congressional Fellowship Committee folder, Donald A. Ritchie's organizational files, Historical Office, U.S. Senate [hereafter cited as "Ritchie files"]).

93. Melvin Kranzberg to Mack Thompson, 7 April 1980 (AHA Congressional Fellowship folder, correspondence series, Melvin Kranzberg papers, National Museum of American History Archives Center, Washington, D.C. [hereafter cited as "Kranzberg papers"]).

94. E. Lee Marmon, quoted in William Poe, "Mellon Fellows in Congress Apply History and Philosophy to Legislation," *Humanities Report* (June 1981), p. 8.

95. Melvin Kranzberg to Mack Thompson, 17 April 1981 (American Historical Association folder, correspondence series, Kranzberg papers).

96. David W. Reinhard, "The Congressional Fellowship: Public Policy and the Hill," *AHA Perspectives*, 21 (January 1983), 24.

97. See Poe, "Mellon Fellows in Congress Apply History and Philosophy to Legislation," pp. 8-11.

98. Timothy Lynch quoted in ibid., p. 11.

99. See John O'Connor to Samuel Gammon, 2 December 1981; and O'Connor to Gammon, 13 October 1982 (Congressional Fellowship Program/ Grants folder, AHA files).

CHAPTER 4 ENDNOTES

100. Samuel R. Gammon to John O'Connor, 8 December 1981 (Congressional Fellowship Program/Grants folder, AHA files).

101. American Historical Association and American Philosophical Association, "Joint Proposal to the Andrew W. Mellon Foundation for Continued Program of Congressional Fellows" [undated; probably mid-October 1982] (Congressional Fellowship Program/Grants folder, AHA files).

102. Samuel R. Gammon to Laurence D. Stifel, 14 October 1982 (Congressional Fellowship Program/Grants folder, AHA files).

103. Samuel R. Gammon to Alberta Arthurs, 6 August 1985 (Final Report/Rockefeller Congressional Fellowship folder, AHA files).

104. See Martha H. Swain, Report of the Committee on Congressional Fellowships—1984 [undated] (AHA Congressional Fellowship Committee folder, Ritchie files). For his observation about declining numbers of fellowship applications having no effect on the persistently high quality of the applicants, see Melvin Kranzberg to Samuel Gammon, 14 March 1983 (American Historical Association Congressional Fellowship Committee folder, correspondence series, Kranzberg papers).

105. Donald A. Ritchie to Samuel R. Gammon, 15 February 1984 (AHA Congressional Fellowship Committee folder, Ritchie files).

106. Samuel R. Gammon to Donald A. Ritchie, 21 February 1984 (AHA Congressional Fellowship Committee folder, Ritchie files).

107. Swain, Report of the Committee on Congressional Fellowships. Lois A. Aroian, one of the 1983-84 AHA Fellows, told the historical association in her final report that "while the amount of our fellowship was very generous in the first year four years ago, it is increasingly difficult for single income individuals to sustain themselves in this area." Lois A. Aroian, Mid-Term Report, February 1984 (Final Report/Rockefeller Congressional Fellowship folder, AHA files).

108. Several of these motivations were discussed in telephone interview, author with Jamil Zainaldin, 18 May 1994.

Chapter 5

1. Memorandum, Elliot A. Segal to Richard Scribner, 20 September 1974 (Summary Data/1973-74 binder, box 1, CSEFP Summary Data records, AAAS Archives, Washington, D.C. [hereafter cited as "Summary Data records"]).

2. Telephone interview, author with John Andelin, 30 March 1994 and 4 April 1994; and telephone interview, author with Ezra Heitowit, 16 June 1994.

3. Lee H. Hamilton to John O'Connor, 25 March 1982 (Congressional Fellowship Program/Grants folder, American Historical Association office files, Washington, D.C.)

4. Memorandum, Ben Cooper to Richard Scribner, 28 October 1974 (Summary Data/1973-74 binder, box 1, Summary Data records).

5. Jerome Paul Harper, Final Report, 28 August 1975 (Summary Data/1974-75 binder, box 1, Summary Data records).

6. Telephone interview, author with Richard A. Scribner, 28 September 1993.

7. Appendix C lists the entire range of offices that hosted and competed for Congressional Science and Engineering Fellows.

8. Interview, author with John D. Holmfeld, 8 September 1993. Ken Hechler, *Toward the Endless Frontier: History of the Committee on Science and Technology, 1959-79* (Washington: GPO, 1980) discusses contributions of several of the committee's early Fellows.

9. Tom Lewis to Stephen Nelson, 21 December 1990 (ASME folder, box 1, Claudia Sturges Congressional Fellows collection, AAAS Archives, Washington, D.C. [hereafter cited as "Sturges collection"]).

10. David Hanson, "Althuis Completes Year as ACS Fellow," *Chemical & Engineering News*, 57 (October 15, 1979), 36-37.

11. Heitowit interview, 16 June 1994.

CHAPTER 5   ENDNOTES

12. Haven Whiteside, Report on Congressional Fellowship, 24 September 1975 (Summary Data/1974-75 binder, box 1, Summary Data records).

13. Telephone interview, author with Patricia Garfinkel, 25 July 1993. Garfinkel elaborated that she thought the issue of how to use effectively the scientific and technical talent available in the U.S. is a challenge that goes far beyond the Congress to embrace much of American society. The country as a whole does not know how best to use such people, she contends; society lacks an effective strategy to take advantage of these human resources.

14. Interview, author with Albert H. Teich, 21 September 1993.

15. Fred Richmond to Richard A. Scribner, 24 August 1976 (Congressional Fellows/1976 binder, Congressional Response Forms/1973-80 box, Sturges collection).

16. See William R. Moomaw to Richard Scribner, 19 October 1976 (Summary Data/1975-76 binder, box 1, Summary Data records).

17. Cecil Heftel to Charles A. Mosher, 16 August 1979 (Congressional Responses/1979-80 binder, Congressional Response Forms/1973-80 box, Sturges collection).

18. John J. LaFalce to William G. Wells, Jr., 19 August 1980 (Congressional Response Forms/1980-81 binder, box 2, Summary Data records).

19. Robert L. Livingston to Richard A. Scribner, 29 July 1982 (Congressional Response Forms/1982-83 binder, box 1, Summary Data records).

20. Al Swift to A.F. Spilhaus, 5 August 1982 (Summary Data/1981-82 binder, box 1, Summary Data records).

21. Albert Gore, Jr., to Dick Scribner, 17 August 1978 (Congressional Responses/1978-79 binder, Congressional Response Forms/1973-80 box, Sturges collection).

22. Albert Gore, Jr., to Charles A. Mosher, 3 August 1979 (Congressional Responses/1979-80 binder, Congressional Response Forms/1973-80 box, Sturges collection).

23. George E. Brown, Jr., to Richard A. Scribner, 28 July 1977 (Congressional Fellows/1977-78 binder, Congressional Response Forms/1973-80 box, Sturges collection).

24. Skip Stiles to Richard A. Scribner, 15 August 1983 (1983 Orientation folder, box M-U-3 #2, CSEFP 1973-78 records, AAAS Archives, Washington, D.C. [hereafter cited as "CSEFP records"]).

25. George E. Brown, Jr., to Stephen D. Nelson, 21 August 1986 (Congressional Response Forms/1986-87 binder, Misc. Congressional and Diplomacy Program active files, Directorate for Science and Policy Programs, AAAS, Washington, D.C. [hereafter cited as "CDP active files"]).

26. Howard Wolpe to Richard Scribner, 26 August 1983 (1983 Orientation folder, box M-U-3 #2, CSEFP records). (Emphasis in original.)

27. Jeff Bingaman to Richard A. Scribner, 27 July 1984 (Congressional Response Forms/1984-85 binder, CDP active files).

28. Slade Gorton, "Tenth Anniversary of the Congressional Science and Engineering Fellows Program," *Congressional Record—Senate*, 129 (29 June 1983), 9482.

29. Radford Byerly, Jr., to Stephen D. Nelson, 25 July 1986 (Congressional Response Forms/1986-87 binder, CDP active files).

30. See Carnegie Commission on Science, Technology, and Government, *Science, Technology, and Congress: Expert Advice and the Decision-Making Process* (New York: Carnegie Commission on Science, Technology, and Government, 1991), pp. 11, 31-32.

31. N.R. Werthamer, Final Report of Tenure as an American Physical Society Congressional Fellow, 16 September 1974 (Summary Data/1973-74 binder, box 1, Summary Data records).

32. Memorandum, Ben Cooper to Richard Scribner, 28 October 1974 (Summary Data/1973-74 binder, box 1, Summary Data records).

33. See Ronal W. Larson, Final Report to the IEEE, May 1974 (Summary Data/1973-74 binder, box 1, Summary Data records).

34. Memorandum, Elliot A. Segal to Richard Scribner, 20 September 1974 (Summary Data/1973-74 binder, box 1, Summary Data records).

CHAPTER 5 ENDNOTES

35. Michael Telson, Congressional Science Fellowship Final Report, June 1975 (Summary Data/1973-74 binder, box 1, Summary Data records).

36. Telephone interview, author with Michael L. Telson, 9 May 1994.

37. Memorandum, Allan Hoffman to Mary Shoaf and Richard Scribner, 2 September 1975 (Summary Data/1974-75 binder, box 1, Summary Data records).

38. Telephone interview, author with Allan R. Hoffman, 1 July 1994.

39. Lloyd B. Craine to Richard Scribner, 16 October 1975 (Summary Data/1974-75 binder, box 1, Summary Data records).

40. Haven Whiteside, Report on Congressional Fellowship, 24 September 1975 (Summary Data/1974-75 binder, box 1, Summary Data records). Federal City College later became part of the University of the District of Columbia.

41. William R. Moomaw to Richard Scribner, 19 October 1976 (Summary Data/1975-76 binder, box 1, Summary Data records). Frustration of not receiving credit for one's work ran through a small, cross-disciplinary substratum of the entire fellowship program. For example, Lois A. Aroian, the 1983-84 American Historical Association Fellow, observed that whatever publishing the congressional Fellows "can do here is either under the name of our member or is being done in our not-very-spare time." Lois A. Aroian, Mid-Term Report, February 1984 (Final Report/Rockefeller Congressional Fellowship folder, American Historical Association office files, Washington, D.C.)

42. See Annette T. Rosenblum and Mary L. Wolfe, "Congressional Fellows," *Chemtech*, 16 (January 1986), 17-18; and "Barker, Ramonas Enthusiastic about Year's Service as ACS Fellows," *Chemical & Engineering News*, 60 (November 29, 1982), 29-39.

43. Norine E. Noonan's self-description of her fellowship year appears in Rosenblum and Wolfe, "Congressional Fellows," p. 18.

44. Paul Horwitz, Final Report, August 1976 (Summary Data/1975-76 binder, box 1, Summary Data records).

45. Quoted in Hanson, "Althuis Completes Year as ACS Fellow."

46. Quoted in "Eck, Ziman Complete Year as ACS Fellows," *Chemical & Engineering News*, 58 (27 October 1980), 34.

47. John Wiesenfeld, "Congressional Fellowship—Opportunity of a Lifetime," *Chemical & Engineering News*, 69 (11 November 1991), 44.

48. Gerald L. Epstein, OTA Fellowship Final Report, 2 August 1984 (Summary Data/1983-84 binder, box 2, Summary Data records).

49. See David Hanson, "ACS Congressional Fellow Enthused over Work," *Chemical & Engineering News*, 65 (30 November 1987), 37.

50. Cheryl G. Tropf, "Congressional Science Fellowship: The First Three Months," *CBMS Newsletter*, Jan.-Feb. 1981, p. 2 (newsletter of the Conference Board of the Mathematical Sciences; copy in AMS/MAA/SIAM folder, box 1, Sturges collection).

51. Anne Harris Cohn, "The Congressional Science Fellows Program: Is It Worth It to an Academic," *SRCD Newsletter*, Winter 1981, p. 7 (copy in Society for Research in Child Development folder, CDP active files). Cohn later married, adding the last name Donnelly.

52. Ibid.

53. Grant M. Carrow, End-of-the-Year Report, 30 July 1991 (Summary Data/1990-91 binder, CDP active files).

54. Anne Cohn, Final Report, no date [probably fall 1979] (Summary Data/1978-79 binder, box 1, Summary Data records).

55. For a discussion of staff turnover, see Robert H. Salisbury and Kenneth A. Shepsle, "Congressional Staff Turnover and the Ties-That-Bind," *American Political Science Review*, 75 (June 1981), 381-396. For more general accounts of congressional staff, see Harrison W. Fox, Jr., and Susan W. Hammond, *Congressional Staffs: The Invisible Force in American Lawmaking* (New York: Free Press, 1977); and Michael J. Malbin, *Unelected Representatives: Congressional Staff and the Future of Representative Government* (New York: Basic Books, 1980).

56. James E. Evans to F. Michael Wahl, 31 July 1988 (Summary Data/1987-88 binder, CDP active files).

57. Memorandum, Elliot A. Segal to Richard Scribner, 20 September 1974 (Summary Data 1973-74 binder, box 1, Summary Data records).

Chapter 5 Endnotes

58. Ronal W. Larson, Final Report to the IEEE, May 1974 (copy in Summary Data/1973-74 binder, box 1, Summary Data records).

59. William S. Widnall, Report to the AIAA, September 1975 (Summary Data/1974-75 binder, box 1, Summary Data records).

60. Quoted in "Eck, Ziman Complete Year as ACS Fellows," p. 34.

61. See minutes of meeting of scientific and engineering society representatives on Congressional Science and Engineering Fellows, 14 August 1975 [prepared by R. A. Scribner and L. Parfitt on 30 September 1975] (Congressional Fellows/1971-73 folder, box 2, Catherine Borras Second Accession collection, AAAS Archives, Washington, D.C. [hereafter cited as "Borras collection"]).

62. Richard A. Scribner to Rogers B. Finch, 10 February 1976 (Congressional Fellows/1971-73 folder, box 2, Borras collection). The AAAS Directorate for Science and Policy Programs continues to maintain a database on all former Fellows. Its *Directory of AAAS Science and Engineering Fellows, 1973-1992* (Washington: AAAS, 1992) will be updated in late 1994.

63. Salisbury and Shepsle, "Congressional Staff Turnover and the Ties-That-Bind," p. 395. Despite widespread agreement that the reservoir of former science and engineering Fellows constitutes a valuable resource, many observers of the fellowship program concur that lack of interaction by sponsoring societies with their former Fellows is one of the biggest shortcomings of the program. Interview, author with Stephen D. Nelson, 21 September 1993; interview, author with Claudia J. Sturges, 21 September 1993; Teich interview, 21 September 1993; and interview, author with John Andelin, 4 April 1994.

64. Pam Ebert to Serena Stier, 10 June 1976 (Congressional Fellows/1971-73 folder, box 2, Borras collection).

65. Memorandum, Richard Scribner to Members of the Board of Directors of the AAAS, 4 April 1975 (Congressional Fellows/1971-73 folder, box 2, Borras collection).

66. Nelson interview, 21 September 1993; and Sturges interview, 21 September 1993.

67. For results of a 1987 telephone survey of arrangements by these organizations, see Deborah Phillips, "Financing of the AAAS Congressional Science Fellows: Report of Interviews with Sponsoring Societies," draft, 10

November 1987 (copy in Society for Research in Child Development folder, CDP active files).

68. Teich interview, 21 September 1993.

69. Nelson interview, 21 September 1993; and Sturges interview, 21 September 1993.

70. Interview, author with William T. Golden, 21 February 1994.

Conclusion

1. Contributions of Fellows to policy making were often counterintuitive, in the sense that their most important actions frequently involved preventing bad policies from advancing. Telephone interview, author with John Andelin, 30 March 1994 and 4 April 1994; and interview, author with Stephen D. Nelson, 21 September 1993.

2. Interview, author with Albert H. Teich, 21 September 1993. Teich himself had earned a Ph.D. in political science from MIT in 1969, with science policy as his major field of concentration.

3. The tendency of Congress to draw its professional staff from ranks of the legal profession, business, political science, and journalism has changed little in two decades. For more detailed analysis of congressional staffing patterns, see Beth M. Henschen and Edward I. Sidlow, "The Recruitment and Career Patterns of Congressional Committee Staffs: An Exploration," *Western Political Quarterly*, 39 (December 1986), 701-708; Paul S. Rundquist, Judy Schneider, and Frederick H. Pauls, *Congressional Staff: An Analysis of Their Roles, Functions, and Impacts* (Washington: Congressional Research Service, Library of Congress, January 1992); Craig Schultz, *1992 U.S. House of Representatives Employment Practices: A Study of Staff Salary, Tenure, Demographics and Benefits* (Washington: Congressional Management Foundation, 1992); Craig Schultz, *1993 U.S. Senate Employment Practices: A Study of Staff Salary, Tenure, Demographics and Benefits* (Washington: Congressional Management Foundation, 1993); Norman J. Ornstein, Thomas J. Mann, and Michael J. Malbin, *Vital Statistics on Congress, 1993-1994* (Washington: Congressional Quarterly, 1994); and Susan Webb Hammond, "Congressional Staffs," in Joel H. Silbey (ed.), *Encyclopedia of the American Legislative System* (New York: Charles Scribner's Sons, 1994), vol. II, pp. 785-800.

4. Andelin interview, 4 April 1994.

5. John Andelin to Claudia Sturges, 10 May 1994 (Directorate for Science and Policy Programs office files, American Association for the Advancement of Science, Washington, D.C.).

INDEX

A

Acoustical Society of America (ASA), 110
AIDS research and policy, 92, 102
Air Force Office of Scientific Research, 21
Althuis, Thomas H., 62, 84, 101
American Association for the Advancement of Science (AAAS)
   Committee on Science in the Promotion of Human Welfare, 8, 9, 10
   Committee of Young Scientists (COYS), later Youth Council, 8-10, 14, 17, 18
   funding, 35-36, 110
   on integrating engineers with scientists, 46
   Office of Science and Society, 5, 59
   program coordination by, 115
   reform in, 4-5
   see also Congressional Science and Engineering Fellowship Program (CSEFP)
American Chemical Society (ACS)
   Chemistry and Public Affairs Fellows, 60-61
   Committee on Chemistry and Public Affairs, 58, 60, 67, 101
   Department of Chemistry and Public Affairs, 58, 59, 62
   effects of sponsorship on, 108
   Fellows, 43, 84-85, 99-102
   fellowship program, 58-67
   joins AAAS program, 62

   program audit, 67
   and public perception of science, 62-63
   Subcommittee on Public Policy for Committee on Chemistry and Public Affairs, 67
American Geophysical Union (AGU), 46, 89, 110
American Historical Association (AHA), 74-79, 110
American Institute of Aeronautics and Astronautics (AIAA), 107-8
American Mathematical Society/ Mathematical Association of America/Society for Industrial and Applied Mathematics Fellow, 102-3,
American Philosophical Association (APhA), 74-79, 82, 102, 110
American Physical Society (APS), 8, 10, 19, 31, 45
   Fellows, 26, 28, 32, 33, 35, 50-56, 83, 92, 94, 97, 100
   Forum on Physics and Society, 51-52
   funding, 110
   program oversight, 53-56
   work of Fellows, 85-86, 92
American Political Science Association (APSA)
   fellowship program, 10, 11, 14, 20-22, 56, 59, 75, 92
   protests AAAS name choice, 24 25
American Psychological Association (APA), 37-40, 109, 110

185

INDEX

American Society for Microbiology, 110
American Society of Agronomy/Crop Science Society of America/Soil Science Society of America/Weed Science Society of America congressional fellowship, 110
American Society of Mechanical Engineers (ASME) congressional fellowship, 14-17, 28, 30, 46, 84
Andelin, John, 15, 30, 52, 68, 70-71, 114, 153 n44
Antiballistic missile (ABM), 2
Arab oil embargo, 26, 29
Atomic Energy Commission, *see* Nuclear Regulatory Commission

B

Bandura, Albert, 37
Barker, Robert H., 99
Beach, Walter E., 25
Bell Laboratories, 26, 94
Bevan, William, Jr., 4-5, 11, 19-20, 37-40, 69, 72
Bingaman, Jeff, 92
Blahous, Charles, 33
Bloch, Herman S., 58
Boffey, Philip M., 4
Bolt, Richard H., 10, 151 n25
Bolt Beranek and Newman, Inc., 151 n25
Bonds, Wesley D., Jr., 59
Brown, George E., 32, 77, 84, 91
Brunell, Dave, 153 n44
Bumpers, Dale, 87, 98-99
Bundy, McGeorge, 69
Burton, Joe, 10
Byerly, Radford, 93

C

Cain, Joseph C. 46

California Institute of Technology, 27
California Polytechnic State University, 77
Callis, Clayton F., 66-67
Campbell, Donald T., 39
Carey, William D., 40-42, 64, 65
Carnegie Commission on Science, Technology, and Government, 93
Carron, Grant, 103-4
Carter, Jimmy, 31
Casper, Barry M., 51-52
Chemical & Engineering News, 63
Chevron, 44
Child care issues, 30
Citizens for Ecological Action, 21
Clemson University, 99
Clinch River Breeder Reactor, 92
Cohelan, Jeffrey, 6
Cohn, Anne Harris, 103, 104
Committee of Young Scientists (COYS), *see* American Association for the Advancement of Science (AAAS)
Congressional Budget Office (CBO), 32
Congressional Research Service (CRS), 30, 32, 42
Congressional Science and Engineering Fellowship Program (CSEFP)
  assessments of, 81-85
  disciplinary diversity of program, 45-47
  first class of, 25-26
  formal naming of, 24-25
  foundation financial support for, 40-42
  funding for, 13-14, 17-20, 23, 34 36, 109-10
  launch of, 5-7
  long-term program impact, 113 15
  need to orient employers, 86-87
  nonscientist fellowships, 73-79

INDEX

orientation and placement of Fellows, 32-34
personal experiences of Fellows, 93-106
quality of applicants, 18-19, 23
rationale for, 11-13, 19-20
relationship to APSA program, 20-22
relationship with collaborating organizations, 44-47
types of assignments, 87-93
Cooper, Benjamin S., 25-26, 29, 83, 94-95
Cornell, Kevin, 162-67 $n2$
Cornell University, 21
Council on Environmental Quality, 95
Craine, Lloyd B., 31, 32, 57, 97, 162 $n2$
Cranston, Alan, 6
Crum, John K, 64-66
Cunniff, Patricia A., 67

D

Daddario, Emilio Q., 9, 68-69
Davis, Harold, 52-53
Davis, John, 28
Diehn, Bodo, 61
Drayton, William, 18
Duke University, 39
Dundon, Stanislaus J., 77

E

Earth Day, 2, 21
Ebert, Pamela, see Pamela Ebert Flattau
Ellis, Walter, 44
Energy Information Act, 26
Energy issues and policy, 24-32, 57, 88, 92-93
Energy Reorganization Act of 1974, 31
Energy Research and Development Administration (ERDA), 27, 31

Engineering, public image of, 14-17
Environmental issues and policy, 4, 24, 28-32, 88-89, 92-93
Environmental Protection Agency (EPA), 95
Epstein, Gerald L., 101-2
Evans, James E., 105-6

F

Fainberg, Tony, 92
Federal City College, 97
Federal Energy Administration, 27, 95
Federation of American Societies for Experimental Biology (FASEB), 44
Fischer, Karen, 73
Flattau, Pamela Ebert, 38, 109
Fleischmann, Max C., Foundation, 41
Ford Foundation, 35-36, 69, 156 $n64$
Foundation for Child Development, 73, 74
Froman, Lawrence, 38

G

Gammon, Samuel R., 77, 79
Garfield, Eugene, 65
Garfinkel, Patricia, 86-87
General Accounting Office (GAO), 32, 42, 84
Geological Society of America (GSA), 105-6, 110
Georgetown University, 99
George Washington University, 16
Georgia Institute of Technology, 27
Gephardt, Richard A., 102
Glenn, John, 39
Golden, William T., 17-18, 20, 35, 40-41, 59, 111
Gore, Albert, Jr., 66-67, 84, 90-91, 104
Gorton, Slade, 93

INDEX

Grant, William T., Foundation, 72, 74
Gregg, Judd, 99
Gude, Gilbert, 61

H

Hamilton, Lee H., 82
Harper, Jerome Paul, 69, 83, 162 *n*2
Hart, Philip, 83
Harvard University, 8
Havens, William W., Jr., 45, 51-52
Health issues, 30, 90-91
Hedlund, Ronald, 22
Heftel, Cecil, 88
Heitowit, Ezra, 85
Hill, Christopher T., 67
Hoffman, Allan, 31, 96-97, 162 *n*2
Holden, Constance, 31, 60-61
Holmfeld, John D., 84
Horwitz, Paul, 100-101
Hyman, Barry I., 16-17, 28

I

Institute of Electrical and Electronics Engineers (IEEE), 19, 21
  benefits of sponsorship to, 107
  Fellows, 30-32, 97
    fellowship program, 46, 49, 56-57
  funding, 110
IEEE Spectrum, 56
Institute for Scientific Information, 65
Iowa Democratic Party, 26
Iowa State University, 25, 94

J

Jackson, Henry M., 24, 26, 29
Johns Hopkins University, 4
Johnson, Robert Wood, Foundation, 156 *n*62

K

Kelly, Henry, 36
Kennedy, Edward M., 39, 100
Kettering, Charles F., Foundation, 19
King, Andrea B., 102
Kranzberg, Melvin, 75-76
Krasnow, Richard, 47
Kreidler, Robert, 40

L

LaFalce, John J., 88
Larson, Ronal W., 27-28, 30, 57, 95, 106-7
Lawrence Radiation Laboratory, 5
Lewis, Tom, 84
Livingston, Robert L., 89
Love Canal, 88, 104
Lowry, Mike, 105
Lynch, Timothy, 77

M

Magnuson, Warren, 27, 97, 106
Mansfield Amendment, 2
Marmon, E. Lee, 76
Massachusetts Institute of Technology, 27
Mathews, Jessica Tuchman, 27, 154-155 *n*53
McCarthy for President Committee, 27
McCormack, Mike, 15, 27-30, 52, 153 *n*42
McDade, Joseph M., 77
McGinty, Kathleen, 66
Mellon, Andrew W., Foundation, 74-75, 78
Michigan State University, 59
Milbank Memorial Fund, 20
Miller, William P., Jr., 15-16

INDEX

Moomaw, William R., 87-88, 98-99
Mosher, Charles A., 26
Moss, Thomas, 32, 162 *n*2

N

National Academy of Engineering (NAE), 67
National Academy of Sciences (NAS) Committee on Science, Engineering, and Public Policy, 97
National Aeronautics and Space Administration (NASA), 1, 3, 31
National Institutes of Health (NIH), 1
National Research Council (NRC) Commission on Human Resources, 109
National Science Foundation (NSF), 1, 3, 31, 61, 95
National Society of Professional Engineers (NSPE), 110
Naves, Renee G., 60-61
Nelson, Stephen, 43, 46, 64-65, 91, 111
New York City Bureau of the Budget, 27
New York Times Foundation, 156 *n*64
Nicholson, Richard, 64-65
Nixon, Richard, 2
Nonnuclear Energy R&D Act, 27
Noonan, Norine E., 99-100
Norris, William, 71
Nuclear energy issues, 88-89, 92
Nuclear Regulatory Commission (NRC), 31

O

Office of Coal Research, 31
Office of Management and Budget (OMB), 99
Office of Technology Assessment (OTA), 7, 32, 35, 36, 42
  fellowship program, 67-71
  personal experiences of Fellows, 101-2
  placement of IEEE Fellows, 56-57, 83
  Technology Assessment Board, 26, 68-69, 71
Optical Society of America (OSA), 20
Organization of Petroleum Exporting Countries (OPEC), 29
Overberger, Charles G., 58

P

Packwood, Bob, 57
Participant Observation in Studying Congress: The Congressional Fellowship Program, 22
Persian Gulf War, 92
Phillips, Deborah, 74
Physics Today, 52
Polsby, Nelson W., 3
Poynter Fund, 156 *n*64
President's Council of Advisors on Science and Technology (PCAST), 30-31
President's Office of Science and Technology Policy, 32
President's Science Advisory Committee (PSAC), 2
Primack, Joel R., 5-6, 8-9, 14, 16-18, 51
Purcell, Arthur H., 22, 23
Purcell, Ed, 10

Q

Quigley, Stephen T., 58, 61, 62

R

Ratchford, J. Thomas, 15, 21, 30, 52, 153 *n*44
Reinhard, David W., 77
Richmond, Fred, 87

INDEX

Rieser, Leon M., Jr., 35
Rigas, Anthony L., 57
Ritchie, Donald, 79
Rockefeller Brothers Fund, 156 n64
Rockefeller Foundation, 78
Rosenblum, Annette, 63
Rubin, Michael R., 84

S

Sage, Russell, Foundation, 20
Salisbury, Robert H., 108-9
Sapir, Philip, 72
Science, 4, 19, 30, 42, 58, 60, 69
Science for the People, 2
Science policy community, 113
The Scientist, 65
Scribner, Richard A.
    and ACS, 59
    appointed head of Office of Science and Society, 5, 11
    on APS participation, 53
    on child policy Fellows, 72
    on disciplinary diversity of program, 45-46
    on early impact of program, 38-39, 109
    and establishment of fellowship program, 11-14, 19
    on fellowship alumni, 108
    and first class of Fellows, 25
    and funding, 23, 35
    solicits ASME participation, 28
Segal, Elliot A., 27, 82, 95, 106
Shaw, George H., 89
Shepsle, Kenneth A., 108-9
Siegel, Alberta, 73
Skylab, 92
Sloan, Alfred P., Foundation, 40
Smith, P. Gene, 57
Smith, Willis, 162 n2

Smithsonian Institution
    joint exhibit with ACS, 67
Society for Research in Child Development (SRCD), 73, 74, 103, 110
Space Shuttle, 92
Sputnik, 1
Stanford University Medical Center, 73
Stanford Workshops on Political and Social Issues (SWOPSI), 5-7
Stiles, Skip, 91
Strategic Defense Initiative (SDI), 92
Sturges, Claudia, 111
Superconducting Super Collider, 92
Supersonic transport (SST), 2
Swift, Al, 89-90

T

Teich, Albert H., 87, 111, 113
Telson, Michael L., 27, 29, 95-96, 154 n53
Thomas, Gary L., 36, 69-70
Three Mile Island, 92
Tropf, Cheryl G., 102-3
Tuchman, Barbara, 155 n59
Tuchman, Jessica, *see* Jessica Tuchman Mathews

U

Udall, Morris, 27
Udall, Morris K., OTA Congressional Fellowship Program, 71
U.S. Bureau of the Budget, 40
U.S. Congress
    Joint Committee on Atomic Energy, 26, 31
    National Fuels and Energy Policy Study (Senate), 26
    Project Fuel, 38
    research and development patronage, 3

INDEX

U.S. Congress, House Committees
  Budget, 96
  Government Operations' Subcommittee on Environment, Energy, and Natural Resources, 99
  Government Operations' Subcommittee on Science, Research, and Technology, 99
  Interstate and Foreign Commerce's Subcommittee on Consumer Protection and Finance, 61
  Merchant Marine and Fisheries' Subcommittee on Oceanography, 26
  Science and Astronautics, 26, 52
  Science and Astronautics' Subcommittee on Energy, 27, 95
  Science and Astronautics' Subcommittee on Science, Research and Development, 28, 30
  Science and Astronautics Task Force on Energy, 15, 29-30
  Science, Space, and Technology, 84, 86, 97
  Science, Space, and Technology's Subcommittee on Science, Research, and Technology, 43, 84
  Science, Space, and Technology's Subcommittee on Transportation, Aviation, and Materials, 84
  Science and Technology, 31-32, 61, 97
U.S. Congress, Senate Committees
  Aeronautical and Space Sciences, 61
  Aeronautical and Space Sciences' Ad Hoc Subcommittee on the Upper Atmosphere, 87
  Children and Youth, 38, 109
  Commerce, 26, 28
  Commerce, Science, and Transportation, 17, 31, 96-97, 102-3
  Commerce, Science, and Transportation's Subcommittee on Science, Technology, and Space, 99
  Energy and Natural Resources, 95
  Environment and Public Works, 97
  Environment and Public Works' Subcommittee on Environmental Pollution, 32
  Interior and Insular Affairs, 24 26, 27, 29, 87, 94, 95
  Interior and Insular Affairs' Subcommittee on the Environment, 27
  Labor and Human Resources, 38, 103
  Public Works, 26
  Republican Policy Committee Ad Hoc Task Force on Energy, 57
U.S. Department of Agriculture (USDA), 1
U.S. Department of Defense (DOD), 1-3
U.S. Department of Energy (DOE), 97
U.S. Department of the Interior, 1
U.S. Department of State, 45
U.S. Geological Survey, 110
University of Massachusetts, 96
University of Virginia, 26, 74

V

Veigel, Jon, 36
Virginia Polytechnic Institute, 16
Von Hippel, Frank, 5-6

W

Walton, E.H., 16
Washington State University, 97
Wells, William G., Jr., 45

INDEX

Werthamer, N. Richard, 26-27, 35, 94
Westman, Walter, 21
White House Office of Science and Technology (OST), 2
Whiteside, Haven, 32, 85-86, 97-98, 162 *n*2
Widnall, William S., 107-8, 162 *n*2
Wiesenfeld, John, 101
Williams College, 98
Wolfe, Mary, 63
Wolfle, Dael, 4
Wolpe, Howard, 91-92
Women's Health Initiative, 92

Y

Yale University School of Medicine, 27, 95
Youth Council, *see* American Association for the Advancement of Science

Z

Zeiger, Alice V., 102
Ziman, Stephen D., 43, 101, 108

ABOUT THE AUTHOR

Jeffrey K. Stine is curator of engineering at the National Museum of American History, Smithsonian Institution. He served as an American Historical Association Congressional Fellow in 1984-85, working with the House Committee on Science and Technology's Science Policy Task Force. He wrote the Task Force's first background report, *A History of Science Policy in the United States, 1940-1985*, published in 1986. He is the author, most recently, of *Mixing the Waters: Environment, Politics, and the Building of the Tennessee-Tombigbee Waterway* (The University of Akron Press, 1993).